"If you have ever asked yourse[...] thought 'I should be nicer to mys[...], [...]en you will want to read *The Self-Talk Workout*. Rachel Turow has experienced and researched the effects of self-criticism, and her book is written with compassion and a basis in science."

—SHARON SALZBERG
author of *Lovingkindness* and *Real Change*

"Given the prominence of our inner voice in the economy of our mental life, it is very fortunate that we can turn to Dr. Turow's wise and compassionate guidance. Some words simply jump off the page and you can taste the relief contained in these practices. Dr. Turow demonstrates that our inner life is more malleable than we assume, and even a little more freedom around our self-talk can make an enormous difference in our lives."

—MATTHEW BRENSILVER
author of *Teaching Mindfulness to Empower Adolescents*

"In *The Self-Talk Workout*, Rachel Turow provides an accessible, sustainable, and scientifically backed process to understand and to skillfully work with the voice within that causes us so much suffering. Turow's comprehensive examination of the origins and impact of self-talk on the many aspects of our lives—personally, socially, and globally—behooves us to take action with wisdom and compassion for the benefit of ourselves and all beings. And Rachel is a phenomenal writer—clear and easy to follow."

—LA SARMIENTO
guiding teacher of the Insight Meditation Community of Washington BIPOC and LGBTQIA+ Sanghas

THE
SELF-TALK
WORKOUT

Six Science-Backed Strategies
to Dissolve Self-Criticism and
Transform the Voice in Your Head

RACHEL GOLDSMITH TUROW, PhD

SHAMBHALA

Shambhala Publications, Inc.
2129 13th Street
Boulder, Colorado 80302
www.shambhala.com

Cover art: Tokumiyanuts/Shutterstock
Cover design: Daniel Urban-Brown
Interior design: Kate Huber-Parker

9 8 7 6 5 4 3 2 1

First Edition
Printed in the United States of America

Shambhala Publications makes every effort
to print on acid-free, recycled paper.

Shambhala Publications is distributed worldwide by
Penguin Random House, Inc., and its subsidiaries.

Library of Congress Cataloging-in-Publication Data
Names: Turow, Rachel Goldsmith, author.
Title: The self-talk workout: six science-backed strategies to dissolve
self-criticism and transform the voice in your head /
Rachel Turow.
Description: Boulder, Colorado: Shambhala, [2022] | Includes
bibliographical references and index.
Identifiers: LCCN 2021055428 | ISBN 9781611808483
(paperback; alk. paper)
Subjects: LCSH: Self-talk. | Criticism, Personal. | Self-acceptance.
Classification: LCC BF697.5.S47 T87 2022 | DDC 158.1—dc23/
eng/20211217
LC record available at https://lccn.loc.gov/2021055428

For Jon,
Oriana,
Felix
& Joshua

CONTENTS

ACKNOWLEDGMENTS

I am grateful for the many teachers, friends, students, patients, colleagues, and mentors who shaped my self-talk
perspectives. Thanks to Matt Zepelin for your guidance, reflections, and patience during this process; and to Lindsay
Edgecombe for supporting this idea. I received valuable input
on earlier drafts from Marie Leznicki, Julie Schnur, Rebecca
Neipris, Kristina Visscher, and Jon Turow. Kristin Kane and
Melanie Langlois have been my self-talk companions, helping me develop and live these practices over the past several
decades—thank you. I'm grateful for the support and enthusiasm that I received from Andrea MacDowell, Alyson
Bingham, Miriam Hodges, Amelia Romanowsky, L Barbour,
Yelena Neuman, Steven Neuman, Rachel Esguerra, Adrian
Esguerra, Jen Thompson, Danielle Abbott, Elisa Mandell
Keller, Jessica Marshall, Therese Huston, Victoria Dailey,
my parents, my in-laws, and my aunt Jane. Thanks also to
Roger Jackson for explaining the historical contexts of some
of these practices, and to Seattle University for supporting
my teaching them in the present. I received a fellowship
through the Hemera Foundation for a residential meditation
retreat, where I deepened several aspects of my own practice.
I'm very grateful to Dalila Bothwell and to my Mindfulness

Meditation Teachers Certification Program sangha for nourishing my practice over the past several years. Thank you to Jon, Oriana, Felix, and Joshua, who allowed me to devote attention to this book amid everything else. Finally, I deeply appreciate the many students, friends, and others who so generously shared their self-talk experiences with me, and who allowed me to include them in this book.

Introduction: Self-Talk

AS A CHILD in the 1980s, I would hear Whitney Houston's song "The Greatest Love of All" and feel confused. "The greatest love of all" sounded accidental and mysterious: the words expressed that the love was "happening" to her, but they also hinted that some sort of process was involved: "The greatest love of all / Is easy to achieve / Learning to love yourself / It is the greatest love of all." But *how* was I supposed to learn to love myself when I felt pretty much the opposite? Good for Whitney, I thought, but I remained baffled by the idea that it was easy to start liking or loving yourself, as though choosing that attitude were as simple as putting on a new outfit.

I carried right on disliking myself, which took the form of constant self-criticism. It was easy to do. Academic, extracurricular, and social settings each emphasized peer comparisons, and there were always plenty of people who were smarter, more talented, more attractive, and cooler than I was. Self-criticism seemed like it might help me to identify and fix my flaws, to keep me motivated to improve, and to become more acceptable to myself and to others. Instead, the habit of self-criticism depleted me, leaving me worried and discouraged. When I finally wanted to develop more encouraging self-talk—the way that I treated myself inside my own mind—I didn't know how to do it.

After experiencing a great deal of painful self-criticism as a child and as a young adult, I am lucky to have had a combination of personal and professional experiences over the past couple of decades that led me to form a completely different relationship with the voice in my head. Today, I'm a clinical psychologist, which means that I've had the privilege of sitting with hundreds of patients and observing the ways that their self-talk operates and improves. I'm also a research scientist, which means that when I hear a claim about a way to transform self-talk or improve mental health, I hold off suggesting it to other people unless I find some quantitative evidence that it works. I want to make sure that the approaches that I recommend reflect well-designed scientific studies demonstrating their effectiveness for a majority of people. (Show me the data!) And I'm a person who meditates, which means that I've practiced different ways of relating to myself, my thoughts, and my feelings—over and over. In my experience, practice is fundamental. My self-talk didn't improve through insight or willpower but through the repetition of healthier practices.

Being kind toward yourself can seem both essential and elusive. I often hear people remark, "I should really be nicer to myself," but also convey uncertainty about how to get there. The habit of self-criticism is often extremely strong; it's often too pernicious to adjust through good intentions alone. People commonly criticize themselves many times a day for a span of years or decades, to the point where they regard self-criticism as a fixed characteristic ("I'm my own worst critic").

I have a different perspective. Because I've been able to see the impact of treating self-criticism with specific and effective approaches in my own life and in the lives of my students and patients, I know that self-criticism isn't a fixed trait. In the span of my four-week undergraduate classes that require practicing these strategies, my students report meaningful changes in their self-talk. It's deeply heartening for me to read my students' descriptions of moving away from harsh self-criticism and developing a more friendly, caring, and encouraging way of treating themselves.

When I attended graduate school in clinical psychology, I hoped to learn concrete approaches to improve mental health, including treatments for conditions related to self-criticism such as depression and anxiety. However, I noticed that commonly used therapeutic techniques such as challenging patients' self-critical statements myself or asking patients to write down self-critical thoughts alongside alternative, more encouraging ones did not seem to work all that well for many individuals. People are often aware that their self-critical thoughts are painful and problematic, but they find that just deciding to have healthier ones doesn't usually work.

Over the past twenty years, I've explored other strategies for improving self-criticism that rely less on confronting self-criticism directly and more on building healthier habits of relating to yourself. The exercises that I offer in *The Self-Talk Workout* involve training friendly feelings toward yourself, tuning in to daily successes, approaching distress in an understanding yet structured way, and prioritizing and reinforcing healthy behaviors. In creating my versions of these practices and contextualizing them in this book, I draw on dozens of peer-reviewed research studies demonstrating ways to decrease self-criticism. I have endeavored to make these practices specific, simple, and memorable in the hope that practicing them can be concrete and measurable for you— less like vague contemplation and more like doing reps.

I use the term *self-talk* to mean the way that you speak to yourself or treat yourself in your own mind, either involuntarily or on purpose. Self-talk can contain aspects of *self-evaluation* or *self-esteem* (viewing yourself or your actions as good or bad), *self-awareness* (being consciously aware of your thoughts, feelings, and behaviors), and *self-compassion* (the tendency to treat yourself with kindness and understanding, especially in moments of failure or difficulty). I include approaches to cultivate self-compassion throughout this book, but I also describe strategies beyond those usually viewed as self-compassion practices, including techniques to motivate yourself to act in alignment with your goals and values, to recognize small successes, to reduce judgment in general, and to handle challenging emotions. Overall, I focus on reducing critical self-talk (self-criticism) by developing self-talk that is more encouraging, friendly, and effective.

In my everyday life as a clinical psychologist and as an adjunct professor at Seattle University, I see self-criticism emerge as a major theme for most of my psychotherapy patients and students. Some describe extreme discomfort when meeting new people, because they're nervous those people are judging them for the same reasons that they're judging themselves. And on top of that worry, people may berate themselves about how anxious they feel. ("What's wrong with me? Why can't I just relax?") Others question their every move at work—and it doesn't help that so many workplaces now demand monumental output and constantly being "on" to respond to emails or texts. Patients with depression are typically frustrated with themselves for feeling depressed. ("I should be stronger. I should be able to cope.") People often view any emotional difficulty as a sign that there is something fundamentally wrong with them, rather than as a normal challenge of being human. And that self-critical interpretation—being distressed about being distressed—begets more suffering.

It's striking that once the layer of criticism diminishes, everything else gets better, including depression, anxiety, stress, and post-traumatic stress. Self-talk can also worsen addictions or promote recovery. A person might use alcohol or other substances to quiet self-criticism; self-criticism about using can fuel additional episodes; and interventions that improve self-talk can lead to healthier behaviors. Of course, self-talk is only part of the picture of human suffering and healing. Healthy self-talk doesn't solve toxic spills, war, or economic inequality, nor the racism, sexism, and homophobia that can contribute to self-criticism via internalized biases. It's not a cure-all, but healthy self-talk can shift distress to a much more manageable level and create more space to appreciate your strengths and to find joy. Working on your own self-talk, in the manner that you choose, can be empowering. Instead of echoing the voices you've absorbed from others or reflecting other unintentional self-talk habits, the voice in your head can begin to express your own deepest values.

In my own life, the minutes of practicing new self-talk techniques have added up, and their combination has changed my life. I go through most of life actually experiencing it rather than second-guessing my every move. ("Why did I say that?" "Why can't I be more productive?") I'm able to focus on trying to do good work and on nourishing my relationships, physical health, and spirit. I do the best I can every day, in each moment. I relax sometimes. When I do things wrong, rather than beating myself up with self-criticism, I try to make them better if I can.

There are still things about myself that I wish were different; for instance, I'd like to be effortlessly organized at home. But my overall daily experience doesn't feature an extra layer of suffering on top, the layer of self-criticism that arises either in words ("What's wrong with you?!") or as a more subtle sense of not doing well enough. It's a much gentler and easier way of being. But I didn't change simply by deciding to have a new attitude. In the first few years of practice, I allocated at least ten minutes each day, and sometimes twenty. And I used specific techniques—ones that have a great deal of scientific support backing them up.

As I saw positive changes in self-talk have an impact on my own life as well as the lives of my patients and the students in my psychology classes, I became more and more curious about it. I began to investigate the scientific literature on this topic, and I was struck by the degree to which self-talk operates either to worsen or improve a rather wide scope of human suffering. There are now hundreds of research studies demonstrating ways to decrease self-criticism and to improve self-talk, and those research investigations inform the approaches that I suggest.

To find out whether a combination of self-talk strategies might benefit university students struggling with self-criticism, I ran several four-week "self-talk" groups over a two-year period.[1] I invited students to complete standardized questionnaires of self-criticism, depression, and anxiety at the start and end of the four-week period.[2] Analyses showed that students reported significantly lower levels of self-criticism, anxiety, and depression at the conclusion of the group than they had at the beginning, a result indicating that these self-talk strategies can produce meaningful changes in a relatively short period. I then wondered if some students might find it interesting to combine their own personal self-talk practice with an academic approach so that they would also learn about the science supporting different self-talk skills and related practices (and receive academic credit for doing so).

Over the past five years, I've taught four-week "Science and Practice" psychology classes ("Building Resilience," "Mindfulness Skills," and "Developing Compassion") in which students explore the research literature related to self-talk and associated topics, practice the skills in this book, and write about implementing these new approaches. Their poignant descriptions of their experiences with these practices, offered across a range of external contexts and internal landscapes, illuminate how self-talk can indeed improve meaningfully with specific, intentional, and repeated practice. I've included many students' accounts of practicing these techniques—either with permission to use their exact words or else paraphrased when I could not reach the authors—to illustrate the strategies in action and to offer hope stemming from others' real-life examples.[3]

Self-Talk Is Really, Really Important, Says Science

Hundreds of research studies have shown that self-talk plays a meaningful role in mental health: self-criticism worsens depression, anxiety, and stress, whereas self-kindness improves those conditions. One study of 349 individuals, ages sixteen to sixty-seven, observed that people with higher levels of self-compassion were less likely to experience mental health difficulties.[4] Another study of 119 university students found that students who viewed themselves as inadequate had higher levels of depression and anxiety in response to stress.[5] Researchers investigating recovery from severe depression observed that reductions in self-criticism among 518 patients formed the strongest predictor of improvement.[6] A range of other studies demonstrate the importance of encouraging, kind self-talk as it relates to motivation, job performance, relationships, and physical health.

Self-criticism is a trans-diagnostic problem because it spans diagnoses or conditions such as depression, anxiety, post-traumatic stress, addictions, and eating disorders that are usually treated as segmented problems by different specialists and addressed among different patient groups. Self-criticism can worsen or maintain an array of mental health problems. I work with patients who are depressed about being depressed, anxious about being anxious, and judgmental toward themselves for having any challenging emotions at all.

Given the importance of self-talk to mental health and the plethora of good research on it, why aren't scientifically supported ways to improve self-talk more commonly known and discussed? Why does self-talk seem to remain so stubbornly in the "woo-woo" or "pop psychology" realm when the scientific evidence of its importance is so robust? One reason might be that the mental health field is accustomed to splitting up, investigating, and treating problems in particular ways, and it's challenging to change those traditions. For instance, anxiety and depression are often researched separately, although many people are both anxious and depressed. When it comes time to pick an area of expertise as a researcher or a therapist, it is more common to choose one that is well established rather than one that crosses traditional disciplines. Much like it's hard to major in "water" in college (you'd probably have to choose chemistry, geology, engineering, or political science), it's challenging to pick a specialization like self-talk that spans mental health diagnoses, even within psychology or social work programs.

Addressing self-talk does form a major element of several effective mental health treatments. For instance, cognitive behavioral therapy (CBT) for depression and anxiety aims to explore and change "automatic thoughts" and "core beliefs" that often reflect self-criticism, and CBT research studies observe that levels of self-criticism can affect treatment outcomes.[7] Cognitive processing therapy (CPT) for trauma and post-traumatic stress disorder (PTSD) targets self-criticism as "stuck points" in the form of guilt, shame, or self-blame after stressful life events.[8] And mindfulness-based approaches— shown to be helpful for addressing a whole scope of issues including anxiety, stress, depression, chronic pain, disordered eating, and addictions—include a focus on refraining from self-judgment. More recent treatments, including Mindful Self-Compassion,[9] Compassion Cultivation Training,[10] and Compassion-Focused Therapy[11] aim to build self-kindness more directly, and have been shown to significantly reduce self-criticism.[12] At this point, there are several effective strategies available even though many mental health practitioners—not to mention most people struggling with self-talk—may not yet be aware of them.

The Self-Talk Workout: Practice Beats Intention

It might seem that because self-talk is "all in your head," you could just decide to have helpful instead of destructive self-talk and that would be that. I remember hearing the advice to turn down the volume on the negative self-talk in your head and to turn up the volume on the positive voices. (Yeah, sure. Where's the knob?) The popular exhortation to practice "positive self-talk" also seems vague to me, because it could mean anything from complimenting yourself a lot to telling yourself that things will go well. If any of those approaches work for you, great! However, for most of us, it's not quite so easy. Clarifying why you want to treat yourself better and feeling convinced about the benefits of healthy self-talk may be necessary steps toward making real changes, but they only get us so far. Jeff Bezos, founder of Amazon, urged his employees to remember, "Good intentions never work, you need good mechanisms to make anything happen."[13]

The key is to practice and to practice intentionally, using techniques that you have chosen because they seem like a good fit for you and because you have reason to believe that they can be effective. Practice doesn't have to be hugely time-consuming, but you'll need at least a few minutes a day on most days if you want to meaningfully change your self-talk. If you're overwhelmed by the idea, you might take heart by noticing some of the other activities that you perform habitually to improve your well-being over time, like brushing your teeth, taking vitamins, buying groceries, or engaging in physical exercise.

In fact, when you practice healthy self-talk, you are engaging in physical exercise. Both constructive and destructive self-talk occur on a physical level. Self-criticism activates the "fight, flight, or freeze" response in your brain and nervous system, whereas constructive self-talk regulates emotions, enhances decision-making, and soothes the nervous system. Your brain and body operate differently during an "OK, you messed up, but that's a normal part of being human" response rather than a "You're a total failure!" reaction. Through the practice of starting and sticking with your own "self-talk workout," a calmer and kinder reaction becomes more habitual, and self-criticism recedes.

Self-Talk and Self-Esteem

Is self-talk the same as self-esteem? No. Self-talk refers to the way that you talk to yourself or relate to yourself, whereas self-esteem has to do with the way that you *evaluate* yourself (for instance, as good, bad, attractive, unattractive, productive, unproductive, and so forth). Of course, they are related: if you speak to yourself as an adversary, and if much of the content of your self-talk has to do with negative self-evaluations, you'll probably wind up with low self-esteem. But it can be helpful to stop thinking in terms of a high versus low self-esteem framework, because judging yourself in general (either "good" or "bad") can create problems. Evaluating yourself highly (high self-esteem) is associated with happiness and optimism, but it sometimes also includes narcissism, having a self-serving bias, being unable to tolerate negative feedback, and needing others' approval.[14] And judging yourself as inadequate worsens mental health.

Contrary to what you might think, the way to handle low self-esteem effectively isn't to try to boost your self-esteem— instead, it involves reducing the amount of time and energy that you spend judging yourself and comparing yourself to other people. That doesn't mean not noticing or caring whether you're treating other people decently or meeting your goals. But too much focus on self-esteem, whether positive or negative, is a trap. It perpetuates a mindset of self-judgment that often leads to suffering.

I've worked with many first-year college and university students who've experienced a drop in self-esteem during their adjustment to college life. Many students' identities were based upon having been high academic achievers as compared to their high school peers, but then, surrounded by other high-achieving individuals, their self-esteem crumbled. The process highlights what the self-esteem and self-compassion researcher Kristin Neff identifies as key problems with self-esteem:

- it is unstable, because it depends on information from the environment, which can change;
- it involves engaging in comparisons between oneself and others that often leave people feeling "less-than"; and
- it promotes an attitude of self-judgment in which your attention becomes trained on evaluating yourself rather than on enjoying your life.[15]

The alternative is to learn to treat yourself in a way that is encouraging, motivating, and kind but that doesn't emphasize judgment or comparisons at all. With practice, you can learn to relate to yourself not as a judge but as a friend who cares about your experience and who wants to help in a supportive way.

Who Is This Book For?

Struggles with self-talk are incredibly common, but that doesn't mean they're all the same. Often, it's a matter of degree. You can think of self-talk challenges as arising in quantities of small, medium, and large, and as taking different shapes, including doubting your abilities at work, comparing yourself unfavorably to your peers, or struggling with internalized residue from others' mistreatment, abuse, or "other-izing." Self-criticism might feel constant, like your background state, or come on suddenly as a storm or an attack—either out of the blue or related to a big exam, presentation, social event, or performance. Or you might be approaching self-criticism as a caregiver concerned about its impacts on your partner, children, students, or patients. The insights and practices suggested in this book may help with each category. The following scenarios depict some of the ways that different amounts of self-criticism might operate.

SMALL

You feel convinced that you want to treat yourself with kindness and encouragement, but it doesn't always happen. Sometimes you slip back into old habits of self-criticism. You've probably already thought about self-talk and worked on it to some extent, but your next steps aren't clear. You want your self-talk to get even better, and you've been meaning to work on it. ("I really shouldn't beat myself up so much.") A lot of things in your life are going well, so your self-talk challenges can feel like baffling, unnecessary self-sabotage, and they sometimes aggravate you. Even if you don't go around insulting yourself with words (e.g., "You're so lazy! You're so fat!"), you might have the nagging sense that you're not enough, not doing enough, or not quite as good as you should be. You could use a fresh approach or two.

MEDIUM

Self-talk is a serious challenge in your life. There's a running commentary in your head that evaluates how well you're doing and compares it to an imagined ideal. You've got a "greatest hits" list of things that you don't like about yourself that repeats on shuffle. You think that self-criticism is part of your character and personality. ("I'm my own worst critic.") You're not sure that you'd recognize yourself without your self-criticism, even as part of you recognizes that your self-criticism is excessive. You still manage to get through the day, and even have some fun sometimes, but the self-talk struggle siphons away valuable energy and attention that you could be using for other things. Your self-criticism may contribute to feelings of depression or anxiety, because the negative self-judgment makes you feel tense, demoralized, and overwhelmed. You sort of like the idea of encouraging yourself more and criticizing yourself less (except maybe you're concerned you'd be lazier or less motivated), but you're not sure where to start.

LARGE

Self-criticism is constant and pervasive—it's your go-to mental habit. It feels like who you are instead of something that you do. You've been attacking yourself internally for years, about a number of different things. Feelings of inadequacy and self-hatred are prominent. The things that you don't like about yourself seem like facts rather than a matter of perspective. You don't like yourself and can't really imagine feeling otherwise. You may have absorbed others' bullying, insults, or abuse, even if part of you knows that you were mistreated. Sure, you'd rather not be so down on yourself, but you're also truly convinced that you're deeply defective or flawed. When things go wrong, you blame yourself automatically. The idea of treating yourself in a kind, gentle, or encouraging way sounds truly foreign, and even a bit frightening. You're most likely experiencing some substantial depression or anxiety along with the self-criticism; if that is the case, you may benefit from seeing a mental health provider (such as a psychologist, licensed clinical social worker, or psychiatrist) either instead of or alongside practicing new self-talk techniques.

If you think you may be at risk for harming or killing yourself, please put this book down and call for help immediately (either call 911 or a suicide hotline or go to the nearest emergency room). Even vague suicidal thinking ("It would be better if I weren't around. . . . I just want to go to sleep and not wake up. . . .") should be brought to the attention of a mental health professional. It can feel lonely and awful to be severely self-critical, but people can and do recover with the right tools and support.

AS A PERSON WHO HAS BEEN MADE TO FEEL INADEQUATE OR "OTHER"

Sometimes they're more explicit, and sometimes subtler, but cultural messages abound about the "right" way to look and to be. Family members, teachers, peers, or the larger culture may have conveyed that you weren't good enough. For instance, media representations often highlight a narrow band of acceptance and approval that prioritizes being white, heterosexual, male, cisgender, thin, able-bodied, neurotypical, free from mental health challenges, young, rich, and rooted in the dominant culture. Even conscious awareness about socioeconomic inequality and the damage that ensues from the ways that the media and larger cultures reward those with one set of unchosen attributes with resources and attention—while marginalizing and penalizing those deemed "other"—may not prevent someone from internalizing negative messages. Mindfulness teachers such as Larry Yang have identified this feeling of "otherness" (for Yang, the "otherness" took the shape of both his cultural background and his sexuality) as both a source of great pain and as a starting point for intentionally building a new, self-chosen way of relating to themselves in a kind manner.[16]

AS A CAREGIVER

It can be extremely frustrating to observe others' self-criticism or to try to improve it. You know it's not serving any helpful purpose for them—in fact, it's undermining them. However, just pointing it out ("You seem really down on yourself") or trying to "correct" self-criticism with your own opinion ("Well, I think you're wonderful!") doesn't seem to do much. You might have students who just can't seem to believe in themselves, a teenager who already has entrenched ideas about being "good" at some things and "bad" at others, or a close friend or partner who seems rhythmically drawn to self-criticism. If you're a therapist, you've most likely noticed that self-criticism worsens stress, anxiety, and depression—but you may not know specific, evidence-based techniques that you can use to address self-criticism directly and effectively.

How Did We Get So Self-Critical?

It can seem truly bizarre that so many of us engage in constant self-criticism when evidence abounds that it contributes to stress, anxiety, and depression. How did we get here? Even though it can seem like arbitrary self-sabotage, self-criticism is actually a logical outcome that reflects normal learning processes and survival instincts. There are many factors that contribute to self-criticism:

- *The negativity bias.* Our brains and nervous systems are structured to bias our attention and responses toward potential threats in the environment and to have a more subdued reaction to neutral or pleasant stimuli. The psychologist Rick Hanson describes the brain as being like Velcro for negative experiences and like Teflon for positive ones.[17] Unfortunately, the brain responds by activating its stress responses not only to charging wildebeest but also to self-critical thoughts. To counteract this bias, we need to practice directing our attention toward neutral and pleasant experiences—over and over again.

- *Self-protection.* Being your worst critic can feel like armor: nothing anyone else says could possibly hurt you as much as your own inner takedown. There's a battle rap scene in the movie *8 Mile* where Eminem raps every insulting thing about himself that he can think of—a move that renders his opponent speechless at the mic. But the emotional burden of ongoing self-hatred (anxiety, depression, stress, lowered motivation) is too heavy to wield in hopes that it will protect us from others' criticism.

- *A culture of comparison and "other-ing."* It starts early: Who's the tallest? Who's the fastest? Who's the smartest? Who has the best body? We use grades or points to show who scored the most goals or got the highest grade. We've got beauty competitions, standardized tests and college admissions, music and dance auditions, and performance evaluations at work. Magazines often feature photographs of very thin or fit individuals alongside instructions for improving your "problem" areas. And, as noted above, the culture often rewards those with a certain set of characteristics with more resources and positive attention while marginalizing diverse qualities as "other" and "less than." It's hard not to absorb such messages.

- *Cultural norms about modesty, self-criticism, and self-esteem.* When I was growing up, it seemed as though insulting yourself was part of the female conversational currency, whereas males seemed to be expected to hide their self-criticism. Cultural expectations about modesty or self-criticism may influence how people view themselves.[18] However, self-criticism might only arise in certain situations, or reflect norms about communicating about oneself to other people rather than a person's inner beliefs.[19]

- *Abuse and bullying.* My patients and students are often surprised to learn about research showing that childhood emotional abuse (for instance, being yelled at, criticized, insulted, ignored, or not receiving adequate support and care) contributes to mental health issues in adulthood just as much as or even more than childhood physical or sexual abuse.[20] Self-criticism forms a key link between experiencing emotional abuse as a child and experiencing anxiety or depression as an adult.[21] Whether it's homophobic bullying at school, racial or ethnic discrimination or oppression, or being hurt by a caregiver, it gets under our skin. Even if we know it's wrong, we soak it up, internalize it, and then do it to ourselves. Building new patterns requires new learning—and repetition to counteract years of negative messages.

- *It's a habit.* Mental habits reflect a type of thinking that is "fast, unconscious, automatic, and effortless,"[22] as well as repeated and hard to control.[23] It's understandable to focus on the content of self-critical thoughts, rather than the process through which they occur. However, the *process* of self-criticism might be just as impactful. One set of research studies demonstrated that the process—that is, the habitual behavior—of "negative self-thinking" affected how people evaluated their self-worth to a greater degree than the contents of "negative self-thoughts."[24] The habitual aspect of self-talk indicates that establishing new habits could be transformative. If you've tried to change other habits—like cutting down from three cups of coffee to one—you know it's hard but not impossible. The initial days are the hardest, and then it gets easier. With repetition, the new, healthier, and intentionally chosen habit begins to take on a life of its own, replacing the old one.

Your Self-Criticism Is Not Motivating You

There's one more reason that I think our culture has leaned so heavily into self-criticism. People often believe that their self-criticism is motivating them, that it keeps them sharp, focused, and accountable. When you picture self-kindness or self-encouragement, you might see yourself slacking off— basically being lazy, lying on the couch forever, eating bonbons, and never getting anything done. But the evidence draws an entirely different picture: self-criticism saps motivation, whereas self-encouragement fuels it.[25] You might recall past projects that energized your creativity, energy, or sense of flow, and that didn't require you to yell at yourself to complete them. If you fear that being kind toward yourself might hinder the quality of your work, you might take note of the research showing that people who are kind toward themselves are viewed by others as more competent and attentive, not less.[26]

Healthy self-talk promotes engagement with life (and with tasks to be done) rather than withdrawal. Sure, sometimes it's important to relax or to take a break, but it's also important to make progress in your work and your other life goals. Healthy self-talk doesn't reflect your inner delinquent teenager skipping out on responsibilities; it cultivates your own inner grounded, engaged parent who encourages with loving direction. You can view the process of building healthy self-talk as learning how to be a kind and effective parent to yourself.

Kind and effective. That's a different attitude about kindness than you might already hold (for instance, viewing kindness as soft or yielding). Can you imagine your inner "manager" leading from a place of encouragement? Coach Steve Kerr of the Golden State Warriors makes every minute count during halftime—with the result that the Warriors usually return from halftime to dominate the third quarter. Providing feedback is part of the Warriors' halftime routine, but the feedback is only valuable if it results in improving the team's performance rather than making them feel more discouraged or inhibited. At halftime, the players watch video clips of the first half assembled by the team's assistant coaches, who know that Kerr wants them to emphasize moments that went well. That is, the coaches provide positive reinforcement by encouraging the players to do more of the good stuff that they're already doing rather than trying to avoid or correct what they're doing wrong. Kerr's focus on reinforcing the positive is an intentional and winning strategy. He's managing—directing the team's behavior—from a place that consciously and *repeatedly* prioritizes encouragement over criticism.[27]

Criticism Can Sometimes Be Helpful

Sometimes there is value in criticism. It can be necessary or constructive. Self-awareness can signal aspects of our lives that need more attention, and our critical appraisals can push us to make changes that align our behaviors more closely with our goals and values. Criticism can be a part of that process. And as painful as it is, critical feedback in relationships, from teachers, and in work settings can also help us grow. We're more likely to grow from it, however, if it's presented in an encouraging way.

Healthy self-criticism usually focuses on specific behaviors that are changeable, or on challenging parts of yourself that are possible for you to manage in a different way. The key is that helpful self-criticism comes from a place of hope rather than despair. For instance, if I'm critical of myself for not keeping in better touch with friends who live across the country, I can focus on the behaviors that I want to improve, like reaching out to them more often with texts, emails, and calls. If I'm critical about myself for being disorganized, I can try to find ways to handle it, like setting a timer that reminds me to clean up for fifteen minutes at 4:30 p.m. There are also aspects of myself that I wish were different but are unlikely to change; in those cases, I can try to accept some of my irksome qualities (my sweet tooth, my jealousy) more gently.

It's the tone that matters. If the self-criticism sounds encouraging and kind, and if it reflects your deepest goals and values ("Hey, I think you need to prioritize budgeting this month and spend less time playing games on your phone"), it may be helpful. But it's best to refrain from self-criticism that contains insults or that even subtly insinuates that you're bad, defective, or less-than. ("What is *wrong* with you?") Any self-criticism that attacks who you fundamentally are, without hope for change or at least kind acceptance of your shortcomings, probably isn't serving you.

Adversarial Approaches
to the "Inner Critic"

Within the topic of self-talk, the concept of the "inner critic"—the part of yourself that trains criticism on other parts or on yourself as a whole—has become prominent in recent years. Some people recommend visualizing the inner critic as a specific character or monster. The idea is that if you can picture the inner critic in your mind, you might be able to see your self-criticism with a bit more clarity and perhaps even engage in a dialogue where you practice sticking up for yourself or choosing a different narrator. Or maybe you could even laugh at your inner critic and not take the criticism quite so seriously.

There can indeed be value in observing the patterns of criticism as mental phenomena rather than as facts, and becoming less identified with critical thoughts that arise. It can also change things for the better to put words onto feelings of self-criticism. In the neuroscience literature, the phrase "name it to tame it" reflects studies showing that pairing actual words with overwhelming feelings can sometimes help us to regulate them.[28]

But even if it helps in some ways, regarding your "inner critic" as evil, silly, or a part of you that should be ignored ("Silence your inner critic!") has some potential downsides. Put simply, it fuels an adversarial relationship within yourself. You might be ignoring meaningful information (for instance, self-criticism that reflects a conflict between your values and your actions). But most importantly, disdain for your "inner critics" just heaps on more criticism. You risk getting stuck in the loop of "Oh, I hate this and that about myself. . . . Oh, shut up, you awful critic! You're so annoying and unhelpful! I can't stand myself for being so self-critical all the time." Ultimately, beating up on the inner critic is another form of beating yourself up, and it leads to the same outcomes of stress and unhappiness.

So, what's the alternative? It may seem weird, but along with regularly strengthening your healthy self-talk, the healthier alternative is to treat self-criticism itself with kindness, curiosity, and perspective in the moment that self-criticism happens. Rather than adding more criticism on top by criticizing your self-criticism, healthy self-talk soothes the criticism that's already there and nourishes new ways to relate to yourself.

The Self-Talk Workout, Mindfulness, and Meditation

Is the self-talk workout a form of mindfulness? Yes. Becoming more aware of your self-talk and implementing new ways of relating to yourself are processes that reflect central themes in mindfulness, sometimes defined as paying purposeful and nonjudgmental attention to the present moment. Mindfulness is often cultivated during meditation, the specific time set aside for dedicated practice of mindfulness techniques. Some meditation practices and traditions such as lovingkindness (see chapter 5) directly develop kinder orientations toward ourselves and others. However, many other meditation techniques also seem to reduce self-criticism, in part by training the ability to observe thoughts and feelings without judging them or reacting to them. Although people meditate for many different reasons, reducing self-judgment is one well-established benefit. If you have some experience with meditation, it's likely that you've practiced observing how you treat yourself within your own mind, including your reactions to disappointment or frustration. Meditators often note that self-criticism emerges during meditation (for instance, judging yourself when your mind wanders away during sitting meditation). Using meditation skills to observe self-criticism in a nonjudgmental way, without getting swept up in it, can help it subside. Because many mindfulness teachers have thoughtfully addressed self-talk, I've included a range of their insights and perspectives throughout the book.

Meditation practice doesn't appeal to everyone, and you don't have to be a meditator to benefit from this book. I've also included other methods of shifting self-talk (for instance, *cognitive reappraisal*, or intentionally looking at a situation in a different way (chapter 2), and *behavioral activation*, or prioritizing and reinforcing healthy actions (chapter 4), because powerful changes related to self-talk can occur via several different approaches. However, I am truly enthusiastic about meditation practice, especially as a structured, repeated, and effective way to transform self-talk. It's usually quite challenging at first. Beginning meditators often react in a very self-critical way when meditation is difficult, and they often assume that meditation isn't for them. It can help to reframe self-criticism during meditation. Navigating self-criticism might seem like an impediment to meditation, but it is often a valuable part of the workout. Part of the way that meditation reduces self-judgment is through the repeated practice of gently noticing distraction, boredom, doubt—and even self-criticism itself—without judging yourself for having those feelings. Meditation trains the mind away from self-criticism, because it cultivates the ability to refocus your attention rather than getting stuck in habitual thought patterns.

Healthy Self-Talk Doesn't Mean Feeling Happy All the Time

The Buddhist teacher Thich Nhat Hanh advises that when we know how to suffer, we suffer less. He writes, "If we know how to take care of our suffering, we not only suffer much, much less, we also create more happiness around us and in the world."[29] I like that teaching because it doesn't promise the impossible outcome of removing suffering from our lives altogether. But "much, much less" suffering? I'll take it!

The idea of "positive self-talk" can leave people thinking that they're supposed to be happy all of the time. It can even lead to the perverse result of people being self-critical when they're not happy. But it's healthy and human to have a full range of emotions. In the book *Care of the Soul*, Thomas Moore describes the importance of opening up to a complete emotional color palette, one that includes shades of gray, blue, and black alongside the cheerier hues.[30] Healthy self-talk isn't about painting over the undesirable colors—just handling them with effectiveness and balance so that they don't take over every canvas.

I think part of the confusion stems from the mental health field itself: the message is that if you have an "issue," like anxiety or depression, that means that there's a problem with you that you need to fix. I absolutely encourage people to obtain support and effective treatment for mental health concerns, but I also wish that people (and their health providers) could proceed with less criticism toward unpleasant feelings. Somehow the idea of being a "together" or successful person became intertwined with having zero depression, anxiety, or other challenging emotions. But being human does mean sometimes having difficult or complex emotions. Just as most of us will have a range of physical health challenges over the course of our lives: colds, flus, rashes, sprains, and simply feeling stiffer on some days than others, why would we expect mental health challenges to be any different?

Self-talk journeys are common. Michelle Obama—brilliant, successful, and admired—seems self-assured, but even she went through a process to get there, and she emphasizes that it's a process that she still continues. In her 2018 autobiography *Becoming*, she describes a consistent, decades-long "thrum" of worrying "Am I good enough?" and being motivated by seeking others' approval. She conveys how her worrying was exacerbated by internalizing many aspects of racial injustice, including those reflected in the long-standing adage in the black community that "you've got to be twice as good to get half as far." She recalls being told by her high school guidance counselor that she didn't seem to be "Princeton material," and she describes the energy drain of being the only person of color in Princeton lecture halls and other settings. After she became famous, she felt belittled by questions from the press that betrayed a sense that she was "other." Gradually, she noticed that her self-talk was "stoking the most negative parts of myself." She shares that, eventually, she handled her persistent self-questioning by answering her inner voice. Rather than to let the question "Am I good enough?" linger and to wait for her actions to generate external approval, she began to respond internally to the prompt. Her self-talk sequence became not just "Am I good enough?" but "Am I good enough? Yes I am."[31] Finally, she articulates how this shift in self-talk radiated outward and sparked her intention in establishing programs to improve the health and well-being of young people, especially those from marginalized communities: "Are you good enough? Yes you are, all of you!"[32]

Working Your Self-Talk Muscles

Almost everyone can benefit from regular physical exercise. To be physically healthy, it's ideal to devote some amount of time and energy to working out. We can't change everything: no amount of physical exercise is going to make me grow four inches or get curly hair. But with repeated workouts, we can get stronger, more energetic, and more flexible.

Why does a mental workout seem so much different? People assume that their mental habits are more fixed—that they reflect fundamental traits. That assumption is kind of strange when you consider how much our culture prioritizes learning and education, activities reflecting that it *is* possible to change the way that we think. While it's true that some elements of personality seem stable over time, the evidence is out there that we can change our mental habits. For instance, the book *Altered Traits* by Daniel Goleman and Richard Davidson highlights research showing that specific aspects of mindfulness training can transform parts of ourselves that we might consider to be fixed characteristics—and yield meaningful changes such as being calmer or reacting differently when stressful circumstances arise.[33]

When I started teaching the class "Mindfulness Skills: Science and Practice" at Seattle University, it was summer session, when only some students and organizations were on campus. My first group of students was almost entirely basketball players. My students practiced self-talk skills in the classroom and then took the new practices onto the court with them each day. They reported playing "better and freer than ever" because they were more focused on the current shot rather than "throwing hate" upon themselves for the last one. And they deeply understood the value of sustained, consistent practice, both for basketball and for self-talk. I've also taught self-talk skills to groups of nursing students, who can benefit from encouraging self-talk as they approach learning a huge amount of new information and clinical skills, and to women in the computing industry looking to advocate for themselves effectively, both in their own minds and within their work environments.

Why not try something new to change up your self-talk, especially exercises that will only take five or ten minutes a day? You can go beyond the intention of "I should really be nicer to myself" to legitimately doing the reps that produce mental change. In research spanning a range of ages, professions, and backgrounds, the evidence is compelling that we can indeed change self-criticism and become kinder toward ourselves, and that meaningful changes usually emerge after a few weeks of practice. By repeating specific skills each day, on purpose, healthy self-talk can become your norm and constant self-criticism can abate. Remember that practice beats intention, and that actually doing it matters.

––––––

The next chapters describe six ways to work out your self-talk "muscles." Although this book presents techniques to manage self-talk as individual skills, those techniques can work well together. You can choose only one, or you can combine a few different approaches. For instance, research shows that practicing self-compassion (chapter 5) can enhance cognitive reappraisals (chapter 2).[34] I invite you to choose the two or three exercises that you like best, set a time and place to practice, and repeat. Once you've gotten into the habit of practicing self-talk exercises, you might swap one out for another, or add a new one to your training program.

Scheduling a time and picking a place for your self-talk workout will vastly increase the chances that you'll actually do it with some dependability and consistency. My friend Eli practices his "friendliness" self-talk (see chapter 5) each weekday on his fifteen-minute walk to work. His routine already has a time slot and a geographic location that he can rely on. It might be during your shower, or as you wash dishes, or right after you wake up. It could be on a cushion or favorite chair. However, I recommend not practicing in bed, because the idea is to practice incorporating healthy self-talk skills into your everyday waking life.

Try not to expect results after every self-talk workout; instead, remember that you need a good deal of repetition to counteract years of habitual self-criticism. Even just noticing your self-criticism is a good first step to changing it. In addition to your scheduled "workouts," you can try any of these exercises in this book when self-criticism emerges.

You can do it. It's hard because you're working against your default way of being, against your habits, and perhaps contrary to your assumption that it can't be done. But you deserve the attention, time, and effort needed to train your self-talk effectively so that your self-talk habits become as healthy as possible. Let's get started.

1

Inhale, My Friend; Exhale, My Friend

ONE BLUSTERY WINTER MORNING fifteen years ago, I was the only person to show up for a yoga class. Instead of canceling the class, the teacher generously guided me through an entire private lesson. Her approach was new to me. She wove friendliness and self-compassion into the yoga poses themselves. She suggested that as I breathed, I could infuse kindness and encouragement into my breathing itself by silently repeating: "Inhale, my love; exhale, my love." The idea was to notice my breathing consciously in the moment (telling myself to inhale and then to exhale) and to combine that referring to myself with tenderness, as "my love." The practice was a revelation. I noticed that it could swiftly dissolve self-evaluation. ("Am I doing this pose right?") It also repositioned the yoga movements themselves as arising from a source of love.

I took "inhale, my love; exhale, my love" and ran with it. It became a sort of mantra for me. There's so much, well, to love about it. It's short: literally one breath long. It's easy. It's portable. I started beginning my meditation with it each morning and then sprinkling it throughout my day. I said it to myself in the elevator, in the first few breaths upon waking up, or in moments that felt difficult. It even started to pop into my mind on its own. Saying "inhale, my love; exhale, my love" helped me focus on my breathing during sitting meditation and to remember that the reason I was meditating at all was love—the genuine desire to take good, loving care of my mind and heart.

"Inhale, my love; exhale, my love" helped transform my default self-dislike to a default self-love. When I engage in this practice, I have the sense that I'm building up and replenishing internal reserves of love, both for myself and others. The phrase energizes and encourages me. It's become a sort of container for my inner experience, a key way that I relate to myself. Moments of self-criticism do come, often enough, when I'm frustrated or overwhelmed, but when I remember "inhale, my love; exhale, my love," it helps.

One of the main reasons why I'm including this practice first in this book is that it's short. It can be as short as one breath, and it doesn't take any sort of planning at all. Its brevity has a special appeal: students in my psychology classes tell me that they appreciate how easy it is to remember and to implement. There's no pressure to start a longer meditation practice if that seems daunting. As the spiritual teacher Eckhart Tolle notes, "Just one conscious in- and out-breath, and a different dimension is there in your life."[1]

You don't need to change anything about how you are breathing, besides noticing the feeling of breathing wherever you feel the most sensation. It could be your chest, belly, or nostrils. Once you've found the feeling, you can really tune in to it. Since the idea is to cultivate a steady foundation of comfort, it's best not to jump around by mentally chasing different bodily sensations related to breathing. Instead, just stick to the spot where you feel your breath most strongly.

It can sound like a cliché, but paying attention to the breath, on purpose, is a true workout for your brain and body. Breathing with awareness changes the way that your brain responds to stressful moments, which may help reduce vulnerability to depression.[2] For instance, one study showed that five minutes of mindful breathing lowered participants' heart rate, blood pressure, and self-reported levels of distress.[3] Paying attention to the breath decreases activity in the amygdala, increases activity in the anterior cingulate and prefrontal cortices, and boosts integration between the amygdala and the prefrontal cortex.[4] Activating cortical regions can help regulate stress by promoting a greater degree of purposeful control over thoughts and emotions.[5] Basically, through purposeful attention to breathing, the part of your brain that is choosing to focus on the breath with awareness (the cortex) seems to communicate with and calm down the part of your brain that reacts to fear, stress, and potential threats (the amygdala).

Five Helpful Aspects of This Practice

As I think over what else "inhale, my love; exhale, my love" (or, if you prefer, "inhale, my friend; exhale, my friend"— more on this below) might have to offer, at least five different components of the practice stand out to me.

FRIENDLINESS

Calling yourself "my love" or "my friend" provides a framework for relating to yourself with kindness, friendliness, and encouragement. That feeling of friendliness is spacious enough to recognize that things might be truly hard—even awful. But the phrase helps us access a deep sort of friendliness that doesn't expect cheerfulness in every moment—rather than that fake "just be positive" kind of friend. So, as I silently say the words "my friend" or "my love" to myself, I'm reinforcing the kind of relationship I want to have with myself, as well as the kind of self-talk that can cultivate it.

BRINGING FRIENDLINESS TO THE BODY

A second striking component of the practice "inhale, my friend; exhale, my friend" is that it matches attention to breathing with kind self-talk. It feels like it's getting the kind of self-talk I want into my body, instead of just having it swirl around in my mind. In this way, "inhale, my friend; exhale, my friend" can encourage an embodied sense of self-kindness. One student observed that "connecting 'inhale, my friend; exhale, my friend' to my breath makes me feel like I'm in control of my mind and my body. This compassion practice helps me stay calm and re-center my mind during stressful situations, and I have made it a part of my daily routine."

I recently listened to a question-and-answer session with the mindfulness teacher Thich Nhat Hanh.[6] One participant asked, "How do I love myself?" I sensed that this person was struggling to love themselves, as so many of us do, and that they were experiencing difficulties with self-criticism and low self-esteem. I anticipated that Nhat Hanh's response would involve the mind rather than the body. Perhaps it's my bias from training in Western psychology or my upbringing in Western culture, but I had assumed that a person who thought or felt about themself poorly would receive an instruction about how to think about themself better.

Nhat Hanh's response, however, didn't suggest a way to handle thoughts differently but rather a way to notice bodily sensations kindly. He answered the question "How do I love myself?" by describing how he greets his body in a gentle, loving way when sitting down to meditate: "I have a body. Hello, body." He then described ways to observe bodily sensations, including breathing. Beyond his words, what gets me is the way that he demonstrates how he speaks to his body: gently, kindly, patiently, and with deep respect. It's not rushed. It's easy to imagine how the caring relationship that he cultivates with his body can radiate toward his thoughts, his emotions, and his interactions with other people—toward loving all of himself.

A friendly relationship with yourself may seem far away. Whether you're facing self-criticism or other forms of hardship, it's common to start out from a place of pain rather than a neutral place. Relating kindly toward yourself is usually a learning process that needs to unfold over time. You can build up moments of self-kindness, accumulating them until they become an accessible option—a new way to show up to the daily swirl of thoughts, feelings, and hardships. I take inspiration from Sebene Selassie, another mindfulness teacher, whose experiences have included surviving breast cancer and coping with racism. She encourages that "healing is more than just stopping a disease or condition; it is learning to nurture ease and well-being within our bodies, hearts, and minds in every moment."[7]

BEING IN THE PRESENT MOMENT

A third component of "inhale, my friend; exhale, my friend" that appeals to me is its emphasis on the present moment—this one, very present breath that is only happening right now. There are so many hardships in this life. Relationships can have thorny misunderstandings or painful strife, or they can end. There's illness and death. There's stress from too much work, whether paid or unpaid. Sometimes it can seem impossible to imagine how you're going to cope over the long haul, or even this week, or even today. Instead of "one day at a time," the practice "inhale, my friend; exhale, my friend" invites us to take things just a moment at a time, which can seem much more bearable.

"Inhale, my friend; exhale, my friend" reflects the practice of breathing meditation in which you try to pay attention to the breath (this breath, in this moment, right now) and to return your focus to the breath when you get distracted. But "inhale, my friend; exhale, my friend" is much, much easier than breathing meditation because there's no expectation to keep your attention on the breath. It's only one breath. The technique might have more of an effect if you do it for several breaths in a row, but you don't have to. It's kind of nice not to have any pressure to continue the practice for more than one breath at a time if you don't feel like it. Even one breath can help.

MODULATING THE BREATH
WITH GENTLE ATTENTION

A fourth beneficial component of "inhale, my friend; exhale, my friend" is that the amount of time it takes to silently say to yourself, "inhale, my friend" can change the length and quality of your breath itself. When you're stressed, it's easy to breathe in a quick and shallow manner, or to even hold your breath. Besides the kindness of the words themselves, the fact that it takes a few seconds to silently articulate them can be an intervention all on its own. There's good evidence that breathing deeply can reduce stress, even if it seems sort of clichéd or simple.[8] "Take a long, deep breath" is sort of woven into breathing along to the words "inhale, my friend; exhale, my friend." This seems to hold true in other languages as well, whether you're saying "inspira, amico mio; espira, amico mio" or "吸气, 我的朋友；呼气, 我的朋友."

Sometimes paying attention to the breath can make people *more* anxious. Individuals who experience anxiety or panic sometimes report that breathing exercises make them feel more stressed because they notice even more tension and struggle to relax their breathing. Anxiety can sometimes manifest in a very physical way, such as struggling to breathe. People who have panic attacks marked by shallow breathing or hyperventilating aren't usually helped by focusing more on the breath because it's exactly the feeling of not being able to breathe that is overwhelming. In those situations, it's usually more helpful to use distraction (such as counting backward from thirty or noticing ten new things about the room that you're in) as a route to calm down the breath, mind, and body.

Because "inhale, my friend; exhale, my friend" is only one breath, it doesn't demand a ton of attention to the breath itself if that isn't helpful for you. Instead, the practice can just help you acknowledge the fact that the breath is occurring. One student noted that "'inhale, my friend; exhale, my friend' is the only breathing meditation that I have ever done that doesn't make me feel more anxious than when I began. Breathing exercises have been a longstanding 'failure' in my mind because I start to panic when someone or something else is in control of how I breathe." The goal of this exercise is to offer kind attention to a single breath, without any pressure to change your breathing. If your breathing happens to become slower and more relaxed, that's an added benefit, but you don't need to try to change your breath.

COUNTERING NEGATIVITY BIAS

A fifth reason that "inhale, my friend; exhale, my friend" can enhance well-being is its potential for balancing attention away from the external stress of the moment and toward internal coping. As humans, our attention is biased toward threats, problems, negative feelings, and things that might go wrong. That's not our fault—it doesn't mean that you're a "negative person" or not handling life well enough. It's just how brains evolved. As a mechanism for staying alive, the negativity bias makes us hypersensitive to potential threats in our environment. Although such biased attention might promote physical survival, the habit of focusing on the bad stuff can harm our well-being.

The neuroscientist and mindfulness teacher Rick Hanson advises that shifting away from the negativity bias takes repeated, purposeful training. "Inhale, my friend; exhale, my friend" can be part of that training. The more I practice "inhale, my love; exhale, my love," the more I feel myself strengthening my inner resources. After several years with this practice, I have the sensation that I'm calling upon a muscle that already feels strong and that I can use in any situation. As long as I can breathe and silently repeat words in my head, I'm grounded. I'm calling upon an inner foundation or sanctuary, a place that can sustain me in a way that transcends the stress of any particular moment.

Handling three small kids—who often each make many requests of me in the same few moments—is easier with this practice. Without it, I'd feel much more frazzled as I try to meet everyone's breakfast preferences, perhaps while holding the baby and making coffee and food for myself. But with this practice, the breakfast shuffle is one of my favorite parts of the day. My situation right now doesn't allow for sitting meditation before breakfast, but I can pepper in some rounds of "inhale, my love; exhale, my love" as I complete dozens of breakfast-related actions. I'm struck that even in those intense moments of serving three other beings, this self-talk technique provides some mental and bodily space to take care of myself at the same time. I'm left with feelings of gentleness and gladness.

Core Exercise

To practice "inhale, my friend; exhale, my friend," you can begin by trying to locate the sensation of breathing within your body. When you are ready, you can start to match the silent phrases ("inhale, my friend; exhale, my friend") to your inhalations and exhalations. Or, if it's easier for you, you can start with the words themselves and allow them to lead the way to your breathing. You might observe a feeling of "syncing up" the words and their meaning with your physical sensations. You can also choose to substitute your own variation on "my friend," such as "my dear," "my love," "kiddo," or even your own name. You might experiment with repeating the phrases for a few minutes of dedicated practice each day, and also inserting the practice even as a single guided breath throughout your day. You don't need to change anything about how you are breathing other than paying attention to the physical sensation of breathing and paying attention in a kind way.

Learning to Notice and Move Out
of the Brain's Default Mode

"Self-talk" reflects the mind's constant commentary—filled with self-criticism, worries, and obsessions. It turns out that the flow of that commentary is governed by a network of specific brain regions known as the default mode network (DMN). Even if you didn't know about the default mode network or call it by that name before, it's probably the reason that you picked up this book. That network dominates our mental experience as the "default," and it will most likely continue to chatter on unless you purposefully strengthen other networks through mental practice.

The DMN refers to a group of brain regions that work together when you're not doing much of anything—that is, if you're not mentally engaged in a particular task. If you're just hanging out, walking, doing chores, showering, and so on, your brain's cortex is most likely operating in this particular way. During those moments, the DMN will probably be engaged and playing the current "Top 40" ruminations, much of them about you and your life.

You might be surprised to learn that your brain is quite active when it doesn't really seem like you're doing much at all. Even one of the scientists who discovered the DMN, Dr. Marcus Raichle, was surprised. "It hadn't occurred to anyone that the brain is actually just as busy when we relax as when we focus on difficult tasks," he explained. "When we relax, however, the default mode network is the most active area of the brain."[9]

The DMN focuses on physical survival, or possible threats that seem like they could harm our lives in some way. We worry about tasks that we haven't completed. ("I have to make that dentist appointment and go to the bank.") We agonize about real or imagined threats to our self-esteem. ("Should I include the department head on this email? Will she be more annoyed if I do or don't include her?") The DMN's chatter is quite self-focused. It promotes a mindset along the lines of, "What does this moment mean about me, and about my life, and what's on my mind today?" There may be an evolutionary reason for the self-focus—a sort of basic tendency to monitor life's landscape for problems that could impact us. That mental activity could also be useful in planning for the future. And sometimes a cascade of interrelated thoughts, feelings, and memories can be interesting or valuable. But at other times, we feel stuck. In fact, greater DMN activation is associated with depression and other mental health challenges. Moments when we are fully engaged in a task and have a sense of concentration, engagement, or "flow" can feel like such a relief. During those moments of flow, the DMN becomes less activated and other attention networks become more activated.

The good news is that practicing mindfulness skills, including the practice of setting aside specific time to pay attention to your breathing, can change short-term and long-term mental patterns related to the DMN. My students tell me that once they learned about the DMN, they could start to observe when they were in it, and they learned to shift out of it by engaging as fully as possible with the present moment. Over a few weeks of practice, they could not only notice more often when they were in the DMN but they were also less likely to get stuck in it.

"Inhale, my friend; exhale, my friend" provides a way to interrupt that DMN chatter. It's a reset button, rebalancing attention toward the present moment, and it's available anytime.

It's supportive, not interpretive. As you practice "inhale, my friend; exhale, my friend," you might find yourself inhabiting your body below your shoulders a bit more and hanging out in the usual parts of your brain a bit less.

"Inhale, My Friend; Exhale, My Friend" in the Classroom

When I began to teach this practice to students in my courses on mindfulness, self-compassion, and building resilience, I used the phrasing "inhale, my friend; exhale, my friend." I had the sense that "inhale, my love; exhale, my love" might seem too corny or even aversive to the students, who typically arrived in my classes with high levels of self-criticism and little experience being kind to themselves. I was also aware of research literature demonstrating that fears of self-compassion and attachment to self-criticism can form powerful obstacles to compassion training.[10] It's tough when you have one go-to mental habit—being your own worst critic—and some well-meaning friend or teacher tells you to try to change it.

So, I decided to present the modified phrase "inhale, my friend; exhale, my friend" as a suggested practice, with the instruction that students could feel free to change "my friend" to "my love," "my dear," their own name, or any self-identifier said in a kind way. I also reminded them to use languages other than English if they prefer. And I invited my students to curiously investigate: What does it feel like to call yourself a friend?

"Inhale, my friend; exhale, my friend" has become one of the most popular practices among my students. It isn't for everyone: some students say that they don't feel right speaking to themselves in the third person, or they indicate that they prefer other practices. Some say that the phrase is "still kind of foreign and still takes some getting used to." But many students identify it as one of the most helpful practices that they learn in my classes. During the final class meeting, they often list it on their "Ongoing Practice Plan" assignment as a technique that they plan to continue after the class ends.

One of the main benefits that students describe is that "inhale, my friend; exhale, my friend" helps them regulate stress and other difficult emotions. One student wrote, "I feel more peaceful after I practice this. I'm much less angry and less easily frustrated." Another student observed how the practice helped ease anxiety while playing sports: "I used 'inhale, my friend; exhale, my friend' right before a penalty kick, and it actually calmed me down!" And finally, a third student commented that "I have practiced 'inhale, my friend; exhale, my friend' quite often recently, and it has shifted my entire mindset as I start finals week."

Students also describe "inhale, my friend; exhale, my friend" as helpful for easing self-critical tendencies. For instance, one person noted that "I'm a perfectionist when I'm weight-lifting and on the court. I talked to myself as a 'friend' because I get really upset when I don't perform as well as I think I should. My positive self-talk turned out to make me perform better. I didn't get so down on myself."

A Radical Self-Talk Reset

I think of "inhale, my friend; exhale, my friend" as a radical self-talk reset—but that doesn't mean it's easy or immediate. It might feel easier for you to connect more with one side of this practice (the breathing) or the other (the self-talk). You might notice and experiment first with the part that feels easier, but also pay attention to the part that feels more difficult. If you've spent years or decades rushing through life trying to be better and to accomplish things, there can be an adjustment period when you finally slow down and reconnect with your body. It might even be uncomfortable, physically or emotionally, to reconnect.

You might consider what kind of connection you have with your body. It's common to not notice much about your body if it doesn't hurt, or even to disconnect from it as a way to escape. Thich Nhat Hanh points out that people often feel alienated from their bodies or find them hard to inhabit because of difficult memories, judgment, or pain. "It is very important to go back to our body and show our concern, attention, and love," he writes. "Our body might be suffering. It might have been abandoned for a long time. That is why we generate the energy of mindfulness and go back to embrace our body. This is the beginning of the practice of love."[11]

Over the course of your life, plenty of subtle and not-so-subtle currents impact your breathing habits and contribute to your self-talk. What criteria for being "a success" have you absorbed? Have you felt affirmed by the ways your teachers, managers, and health providers treated you, or have you felt disrespected? Are important facets of your experience well represented in movies, TV, and other media, or not so much? Over time, numerous messages about what parts of you are acceptable or not acceptable sink in, even if those messages are wrong. It's very hard to breathe comfortably, to inhabit this moment, and to befriend yourself within a culture that tells you that you're "not quite right" or even "less than."

I often felt "less than" in high school, where I was a "B+/A-" kind of a student attending the College Preparatory

School (seriously, my high school, CPS, has no other name). My attention was often focused on "getting into a good college," a mindset that prioritized future accomplishments over present-moment experiences and that equated accomplishments with self-worth. The mindset continued well beyond college, as I worked hard to clear hoop after hoop in graduate school. I wanted to become "good enough" not only in my own mind but also in the eyes of future employers. I knew the steps on the career treadmill, but I didn't know how to live with gentleness or contentment, how to breathe in a relaxed way, how to treat myself decently. I was missing a life with myself—rather than my career—at the center.

After graduate school, I began to explore yoga, meditation, and dance as ways to pay attention to my physical body, in an attempt to live more in the moment. At the end of yoga classes, teachers often closed with *savasana* ("corpse pose"), a practice where I was actually *supposed* to lie still. There was one yoga teacher who directed a long "body scan" (noticing sensations in the body, one body part at a time). She guided students to notice each body part in turn, including each individual toe. This felt outrageously luxurious. I could feel part of my brain going, "Each individual toe? Seriously? I've got things to do!" But another part delighted in the permission to just notice, to just be, without working on being better.

Over time, my efforts to connect more with my bodily sensations in the present moment have added up. It's gotten easier, so that I now have this resource even during hard times. I can keep reconnecting with my breath and physical body in a kind way, and especially through "inhale, my friend; exhale, my friend."

"Inhale, My Friend; Exhale, My Friend" in Psychotherapy

As I start a therapy session with a patient, I often tune in to "inhale, my friend; exhale, my friend" as an intention for both of us. I aim to listen openly, without trying to fit an individual's experience into a category. I see the therapy room as a place of expansion—letting be—rather than one of contraction or holding in. When I've introduced "inhale, my friend; exhale, my friend" to patients, I've heard some interesting responses. Patients have shared that the practice can help them remember to breathe more slowly and deeply, that it can keep them grounded even in oppressive environments, and that it can build self-kindness into their daily lives.

Sitting across from psychotherapy patients struggling with depression, anxiety, or trauma, I often notice that their upper bodies look like statues—barely breathing. I observe tiny oscillations in people's shirts or sweaters that suggest many short, small breaths taking place higher up in the body (shoulders, chest) instead of deeper, larger breaths lower down in the body (ribs, abdomen). It's hard to breathe in a relaxed way if you feel overwhelmed or anxious. If you've had to cope with unsafe situations, you may have lingering physical sensations of constriction. I feel compassion for people who have endured the kinds of stressful experiences that generate both emotional and physical strain. In many cases, I introduce working with the breath as a way to generate new internal habits.

In so many environments—work, school, public places—expressing strong emotions is taboo. We literally have to "hold it together," which can include holding our breath. Or, we develop longstanding feelings of emotional and physical tension. I find such relief in having spaces, such as therapy rooms, that invite us not to hold it together—to let it all out, including the breath. Taking a few minutes to notice breathing can pave the way toward noticing feelings in general.

There are a few therapy patients whose careful attention to breathing stands out to me. I've changed their names and some of their details here to protect their privacy.

JERRY: BREATHING WITH EMOTIONAL NUMBNESS

Jerry was a Vietnam veteran in his late sixties. He made it through the war, but he covered up his feelings with alcohol for decades afterward. Even though he had quit drinking a few years before I met him, he still felt numb. He explained that he couldn't seem to detect any of his own emotions, and he worried that he just didn't have the ability to feel anything anymore. Jerry was regretful that he hadn't been more emotionally present when his children were growing up and confused about how he could connect more with them as adults. He hadn't been in therapy before, but his primary care doctor had referred him after hearing Jerry wonder aloud why he couldn't seem to feel any emotions at all.

Jerry's experience of feeling cut off from emotions is common after trauma. In highly stressful environments, it's often self-protective not to be so aware of your feelings. Over time, that coping strategy (whether initiated on purpose or unconsciously) can become a habit, as it did for Jerry. Because alcohol can numb painful feelings, it's a popular form of self-medicating. But Jerry's pattern of distancing himself from his feelings had built a wall that also distanced him from other people.

As I sat with Jerry in his therapy sessions, I knew that my goal was to help him tune in to his feelings. Building awareness of physical sensations is often easier than building awareness of emotions. It's more straightforward to pay attention to something that's happening right now, in this moment, than it is to pinpoint an emotion that might feel vague or hard to access, or that is related to distant experiences and memories. I invited Jerry to find his breath and to gently focus on the feeling of breathing.

He and I started our sessions with five to ten minutes of breathing. The intention for this practice was to notice the physical sensations of breathing, without necessarily changing anything about how he was breathing. This was a new practice for him, and it proved powerful. He described feeling calmer, and he noticed that he enjoyed the breathing practice. The practice became self-reinforcing for him. I didn't have to suggest or encourage him to practice it, as he became eager to start our sessions this way.

After several sessions of breathing with awareness, Jerry's upper body seemed less rigid. Little by little, over the course of about eight therapy sessions, he began to notice more feelings of warmth toward his children, and to explore his guilt a little more deeply. He described the disconnect between the parent he wished he had been and the parent that he had actually been, and he noted a sense of grief and loss about having missed out. As he began connecting with more of his feelings about his children and about being a parent, those relationships shifted. I never got the whole story about what changed and how, because my Veterans Affairs assignment rotated to the next service, but I remember the voicemail that he left me. He thanked me for our work together and stated, "You helped me become a better person."

MARTIN: BREATHING WITH
REJECTED IDENTITIES

Martin was adopted from Korea as a baby, and he was raised in a predominantly white American community. He'd tried his best to fit in, even though he always felt "wrong." He didn't see people who looked like him on TV or in the movies, or in his class at school. Other kids would ask him where he was *really* from. When he began to realize that he was gay, he tried to stifle his feelings. It just seemed like too much—another aspect of himself that was "other." Although his adoptive parents had indicated that they would be supportive, he had uncles, aunts, and peers whom he knew were homophobic. By the time we met in his mid-thirties, he had found a career that interested him, and he had a wonderful boyfriend. He explained that he felt accepting of his identity, but that he still seemed to worry about many things, including whether he really "deserved" to be with his boyfriend.

As I sat across from Martin, I pointed out that I hardly saw any breathing-related movement at all. He acknowledged that he commonly held his breath, as though even within his own body he was constricting who he was and not allowing himself to just "be." I encouraged him to notice his breathing and any related physical sensations, and to observe any connections to his emotional dynamics. I invited him to be curious: What did it feel like physically when he worried? What was happening with his breath? Did he notice specific places where he seemed to hold his breath or where it seemed stuck? Could he experiment with allowing more movement—not forcing it but inviting his breath to take up all the space that it needed, with no limits? And could he relate to himself and to his breathing kindly?

At first, Martin found it frustrating to attend to his breathing. The tension in his body was such a strong habit that it seemed almost more stressful to notice it. I encouraged him to be gentle with that frustration, and to perhaps think of his breathing pattern as having many subtle components rather than one monolithic idea that he was "breathing wrong." Was there a part of his breathing that felt okay rather than stressful to observe? He noted that the sensations in his shoulders and chest were unpleasant but that the flow of air in and out of his nostrils felt neutral. Over time, he was able to notice a bit more. Once he got used to checking in with the rest of his body, he began to feel less judgmental toward himself for feeling tense. ("Yep, there's that same tension again.")

Martin and I didn't spend all of our time addressing his breath. We also made room for him to express some of his feelings about his early life experiences and the ways that they had affected him. I emphasized how logical it was that he felt anxious, because his environmental context had been so non-affirming. It made sense that he absorbed the pervasive racism and heterosexism around him, to the point that even if his adult, intellectual self knew that it was "okay" to be Korean American and gay, it still might not feel like it was okay. I let him know that I viewed this challenge as affecting Martin but not originating with him. That is, I explained that I didn't see it as "Martin's anxiety and trouble breathing" but rather considered the problem to be "a culture where being white and straight is seen as 'normal' or 'preferable,' (that is, a racist and homophobic culture) hurts people, including Martin."

As Martin shared more of his thoughts and experiences, I pointed out how layered and complex they were, and how his feelings depended on the context and the moment. Being gay felt like not such a big deal in Seattle, but a huge deal in his hometown. When he attended a college summer program for Korean American youth, his cultural experience was the norm rather than the exception. I wondered if he could bring some of that awareness of complexity to working with his breath. That is, instead of thinking of the breath as "good/relaxed" versus "bad/tense," could he try to notice his breathing without judgment? How about tuning in to other aspects of breathing besides relaxation and tension, like the temperature of the air in his nostrils, or the movement of his body against his clothing as he breathed?

Over the course of our work together, Martin's words and breath seemed to flow more easily. He spoke more expansively, without my providing so many prompts or questions. He recounted an incident at a gay pride parade where he and his boyfriend were accosted by members of a church who tried to tell him that it was wrong to be gay. ("I'm just concerned about your soul.") He said that he ended the conversation by saying, "I don't agree, and you're disrespecting me." He reported that even as the conversation was happening, he was tuning in to the sensations of his own breath moving in his body. "I owned my life and my body, and she didn't," he said. His breathing space and his self-kindness were by no means a complete solution to homophobia, but in the moment, they provided some refuge.

ERIKA: BREATHING WITH ANXIETY

"I've been walking on eggshells almost my entire life," explained Erika at the start of our first session together. A woman in her late twenties, she considered herself to be "a very anxious person." Her body language was physically contracted; she appeared to be taking up the smallest amount of space on the couch that she could. As she shared her feelings and her story, she cried at times, and then apologized for crying. (This is a common exchange in therapy. I assure folks that it's absolutely okay to cry, but most people still express discomfort or embarrassment about it.)

Erika explained that her childhood and early adulthood were lived in homes where she didn't feel safe. She remarked that her parents had been "good people" but that they hadn't known how to cope with stress. Even though the family was wealthy, her parents' business underwent fluctuations in profits that shaped their moods and parenting. She recounted that when business was good, her parents were indulgent and relaxed. But when it wasn't going well, they would yell at their children constantly, occasionally hit her or her siblings, criticize them about "everything," or else withdraw from the kids. Erika clarified that she'd only put the patterns together as a teenager, and that beforehand, she'd existed in an environment where "you never knew what you were going to get."

She learned to be hyperaware of small signals: the way her mother opened a door, the precise sound of her father's step on the stair. She explained that those cues could buy her a few seconds to try to "disappear" or at least know not to ask her parents for anything. "I forged all of their signatures on school forms," she recalled, "because when they were in a bad mood, I couldn't bother them with anything." Erika remembered wishing she were invisible or that she could run away. She eventually did escape by moving in with her boyfriend, but soon after they moved in together, he became controlling.

After a few years on her own following the end of that relationship, Erika said that she now felt as though she was in a healthy relationship but that she still couldn't relax. She explained that she didn't consider herself to have any "real problems" in her life right now besides feeling very anxious, and she blamed herself for not being able to make the anxiety go away. Erika reported having two or three alcoholic drinks per night, and she expressed her wish to find another way to calm down.

Many patients who declare that they've "just always been an anxious person" also describe growing up in unstable or unsafe homes. I'm pretty blunt about it when I challenge their sense that anxiety is part of their character, because I see it as a consequence of their conditioning. I say something like, "I'll just put it out there that I don't think that you're an anxious person. I actually think about it a different way. People learn from their environments, and yours taught you to be anxious. It was a smart habit to develop at the time, but it's a habit. It might feel like your identity, but it's actually not a fixed feature of who you are."

Erika seemed to both appreciate and doubt this reframing, but she was open to considering the different evidence-based strategies for anxiety that I listed: psychotherapy, medication, physical exercise, mindfulness meditation, and self-compassion. She said she had been interested in trying meditation for a while but that she didn't know how to get started. Self-compassion also appealed to her because it might help her change "being so down on myself."

We explored the different ways that she could set up a meditation practice. She eventually settled on twenty minutes per day, before dinner. She found a guided breath-based meditation track, and she also infused a few rounds of "inhale, my friend; exhale, my friend" to help keep a kind, friendly, and nonjudgmental focus. After a month or two, Erika said that she didn't necessarily feel less anxious per se, but that she felt "more accepting and gentle about my anxiety." We discussed how paradoxical it is that trying too hard to calm down often produces more anxiety, whereas noticing anxiety gently can have a calming effect. She also started noticing more evenings when she didn't consume any alcohol.

ROOTS OF BREATHING WISDOM

The idea of combining attention to the breath with self-kindness isn't new. Of course, these ideas are often taught separately, and I myself teach a class called "Mindfulness Skills" and another called "Developing Compassion." There is, however, a fair amount of overlap between the classes, even if the themes are approached from different angles. Once you begin noticing how you relate to yourself, to others, to your experiences, and to the world, it's natural to explore *and* adjust how you relate to them.

Paying attention to the breath on its own is a practice that can be so powerful as to be its own path toward growth—and some would say, toward enlightenment. The practice of "inhale, my friend; exhale, my friend" is meant to be a reset button or starting point. I myself have found it a nourishing and transformative practice over the past decade. I've also combined it with other forms of meditation. For instance, I begin sessions of sitting meditation with several minutes of "inhale, my love; exhale, my love," and then I transition to taking my breath as the primary object of focus. Even as I switch over to mostly attending to the breath, I still try to focus on it in a kind and gentle way, and to kindly return my focus to the breath when I become distracted.

The classical Buddhist text the *Anapanasati Sutta* (*Discourse on the Full Awareness of Breathing*) provides guidance on how to pay attention to breathing. These words are thought to reflect the Buddha's instructions—or, at least, what he found to be the path to his own enlightenment. The text introduces the idea with the question, "Now how is mindfulness of in-and-out breathing developed and pursued so as to be of great fruit, of great benefit?"[12] The following phrases from the sutta, as translated by Thich Nhat Hanh and included in his book *Breathe, You Are Alive! The Sutra on the Full Awareness of Breathing*, are offered to enhance focus on breathing and the body with this kind of attention:

Breathing in, I know I am breathing in.
Breathing out, I know I am breathing out.

Breathing in, I am aware of my whole body.
Breathing out, I am aware of my whole body.

Breathing in, I calm my whole body.
Breathing out, I calm my whole body.[13]

There are many ways to weave kindness into breathing with awareness. For instance, Thich Nhat Hanh suggests practicing with the words, "Breathing in, I am aware of my body. Breathing out, I smile to my body."[14] He explains, "This is a smile of awareness, a smile that shows your concern and loving kindness." Nhat Hanh encourages us to relate to our bodies tenderly while breathing in and breathing out, with an attitude of taking good care of ourselves, in a manner that is relaxed, loving, and attentive. If you want to explore more deeply how to focus attending to the breath, and how to develop this practice, there are some excellent guides for doing so.[15]

Some practices involve not only becoming aware of the breath but also changing your breathing in different ways. I haven't highlighted those practices here because the exercise "inhale, my friend; exhale, my friend" is about noticing your breath in a kind, friendly way rather than trying to adjust it. Some people find that trying to change their breathing makes them feel more anxious than just noticing it. But other people do respond well to exercises and techniques to lengthen their breathing or to breathe in specific rhythms or patterns. If you want to explore them, you might investigate either *breathing retraining* (a set of exercises to engage the belly or diaphragm) or *pranayama* (yoga breathing exercises to improve energy or decrease stress).

But if more breathing-focused practices aren't your thing, or if you don't feel like exploring meditation at this point or ever, that's okay. You can use "inhale, my friend; exhale, my friend" on its own, or combine it with other approaches that you find helpful. Or, you can move on to other nonbreathing self-talk exercises included in this book or elsewhere.

Repetition is important with any self-talk exercise. Remember, self-criticism and other default mental habits became powerful because we have repeated them over and over, whether on purpose or not (probably not). To change them, find one or two new things to do, and repeat, repeat, repeat. It's the repetition of small changes over time that transforms self-talk.

REFLECTION QUESTIONS

1. What is your initial reaction to calling yourself "my friend," "my dear," or "my love"? If you practiced the exercise, did your response to those words change in any way?

2. How does it feel to connect with the physical sensations of breathing? Do you notice places of tension or discomfort? Do you notice places in your body where you don't feel much of anything at all? Or places of comfort or ease?

3. Can you catch yourself in the default mode network (the habitual mental commentary that arises when you're not doing much of anything)? What happens when you try to shift your attention toward connecting with your breath and body?

4. Does "inhale, my friend; exhale, my friend" or your preferred variation get more comfortable with practice?

2

Spot the Success

IF YOU'RE A PERSON who makes to-do lists, you're likely to agree with what most people identify as their favorite part: crossing things off. In fact, many people say that they add tasks that they've already completed just so that they can cross off more items. There's a satisfying feeling in checking that box or drawing a line through a task. It's a moment to pause, to stay with the feeling of successful completion. It can also be an energizing moment, one that zings with a sense of confidence, effectiveness, and momentum.

I think of that moment of savoring a newly crossed-off to-do-list item as "spotting the success." As a self-talk strategy, "spot the success" takes this process far beyond your to-do list by challenging you to consciously notice and celebrate many more of your own positive actions, including those that seem unremarkable or insignificant. Directing your attention to a range of successes can help you view yourself and your actions with appreciation rather than disapproval. Over the years, my psychology students have reflected that repeated practice with spot the success has led them to feel better about themselves, more peaceful, more motivated, more mindfully present in their activities, and more accomplished. One person commented that the practice "made me feel accomplished and grateful, even on bad days."

I want to acknowledge right away that praising yourself for what don't really seem like "successes" could seem like a bizarre or silly idea. When they hear about spot the success for the first time, my students often report feeling some resistance. Some students convey that it just doesn't feel like "them" to celebrate minor accomplishments. I appreciate the desire to have self-talk feel genuine, but I also encourage people to stay open to trying out new approaches, even those that don't at first feel quite like "you." Other students balk at the idea of praising themselves repeatedly, in part out of concern that it could cause them to become "full of themselves" or conceited. However, spot the success won't make you conceited, no matter how much you practice it. The exercise doesn't suggest that you comment about how wonderful you are for completing these tasks, and it doesn't impart that you're better than other people. The spot-the-success exercise encourages you to note facts rather than your feelings about what you did—for instance, noting that you did, in fact, remember to mail a letter. The skill helps balance your attention so that you consciously recognize more of your own positive actions.

Spotting your successes can counteract excessive self-criticism. It's natural to pay attention to what you wish were different or to agonize about the gulf between what you've accomplished and what you hope to achieve. That thinking style reflects the brain's negativity bias: the tendency to ignore what's going right and to focus only on what's going wrong. The negativity bias toward ourselves and our own actions can result in feeling overwhelmed or as though we're not doing enough or we're not good enough. However, only noticing what isn't going well is an incomplete perspective; we're only seeing part of the picture. It's also linked with feeling depressed.[1] The repeated practice of spotting successes on purpose can recalibrate attention, thereby decreasing self-criticism and enhancing well-being.

Spot the success is also a helpful strategy if you are struggling to feel motivated or to establish new behaviors. Animal trainers and product marketers know that reinforcing behaviors that are already going well, including the first steps toward a new behavior, helps those behaviors develop and continue. That's why businesses that offer a rewards-club card make sure that the first box is stamped: it sends the message that "you're already on your way!" Teachers sometimes implement "positive behavior management," in which they compliment students who are already demonstrating positive behaviors ("Rachel, you've been paying really great attention to the lesson today!") rather than calling out those who aren't. In a similar fashion, spot the success provides a specific strategy to encourage even more of your own positive actions and perceptions. One student commented that, "It felt trivial when I started, but as time passed, it made me feel as though my days were valuable and productive. It also helped when I felt unmotivated because it would show me how much I actually did and sometimes motivate me to do even more."

One of the main ways that I teach spot the success is as an exercise in which you think of several completed actions that benefited you, someone else, or the world around you, and then write them down, if possible. The invitation is to list ten accomplishments, with no item too small. For instance, you might generate something like:

1. Got out of bed at 8:30 a.m.
2. Did my stretches
3. Went for a walk
4. Showered
5. Dressed
6. Prepared and ate breakfast
7. Texted a friend
8. Sent a work-related email
9. Paid a bill
10. Took medication

While some of these items might seem too mundane for you to have considered them to-do-list goals before, the goal is to practice acknowledging what you are actually doing well, including daily activities. Practicing this kind of acknowledgment can reduce self-criticism and increase self-appreciation and "self-efficacy," or confidence in your ability to take action toward your goals.

I like spot the success because it's an active mental process. Telling someone to just think of something differently is all well and good. You could even agree with the new perspective. But truly adopting a new perspective is much harder. That's why *making the list* is the hack. By actually making the list, your brain is forced to generate lived examples rather than simply imagining an abstract perspective without absorbing it.

You don't have to write the list down, but some people find that they get more out of the exercise if they see the items visually rather than just noting them internally. One student observed that, "When writing down an accomplishment, I perceive it as being more 'real' than if I only think about it. I tend to devalue my successes, because I have a very self-critical mind. Writing all these successes down can outsmart my own thinking and help prove to myself that my day is full of actual successes."

Many people get stuck in the middle of making the list. Coming up with four or five things tends to happen quickly, but then it can be challenging to keep going. Can you stick with it, and keep trying, even if it seems hard to identify more accomplishments? You might also notice how it feels to acknowledge your own positive actions. Do you minimize them, or struggle with the idea of taking credit for them?

You might feel an urge to discount the items on the list, because they reflect pretty basic aspects of life—the ordinary, daily tasks that many of us take for granted. That may be the case. However, they are still meaningful. There's a big difference between getting out of bed and staying there all day. In fact, daily activities like getting dressed, getting groceries, or calling a friend can be much harder when life feels difficult. During those periods, practicing spot the success may help you appreciate your good efforts, provide some degree of hope, and offer an opportunity to notice improvements. Tending to friendships, health, work, and your home all require specific actions, and those actions matter. They often reflect your deepest values. My view is that every positive action can be included in spot the success. Every breath matters, as does every kind word.

Core Exercise

To practice spot the success, write down ten things that went well today and to which you contributed. No item is too small—not even getting out of bed. Even breathing is a success, and it is completely fine to include it on your list. Then, give yourself credit for each success, even if you feel the urge to dismiss its importance.

As with each self-talk skill, its power is in its consistency. You can set an alarm or reminder to practice daily or make a space in your journal. If you feel stuck, you can pause for a minute and dig a bit deeper, as there are always more things that you have done than you might realize.

Redistribute Your Attention toward What's Working

The mindfulness teacher and biologist Dr. Jon Kabat-Zinn reminds people that "As long as you are breathing, there is more right with you than wrong with you, no matter how ill or how despairing you may be feeling in a given moment."[2] Thinking about what's going wrong usually eclipses our thinking about what's going right. However, practicing the skill of noticing what's going right, on purpose, can improve self-talk about many experiences, including physical pain.

Kabat-Zinn began his mindfulness teaching with patients frustrated by years of chronic physical pain. Because their past treatments and medications had not provided them with much relief, these patients had good reason to be skeptical that anything could help them. Several patients nevertheless agreed to try out Kabat-Zinn's eight-week course in Mindfulness-Based Stress Reduction (MBSR), in which they learned and repeated new mind-body exercises.[3]

Kabat-Zinn's patients learned how to notice where their mind went—usually right to what was most painful—and to practice gently redirecting it. One practice, the "body scan" exercise, involves mentally "scanning" through the whole body, from head to toe (or toe to head). Using the body scan exercise, people learned to pay attention not only to the source of their pain but also to other parts of the body. Someone might have terrible back pain but still notice that other parts of the body feel okay, or even pleasant. There might be a particular sensation to notice, like warmth, alertness, tension, or relaxation.

The body scan practice involves redistributing attention. Instead of habitually focusing most of their attention on the pain, people learned to balance their focus so that their scope of attention became attuned to a wider spectrum of stimuli. After an eight-week MBSR course that includes the body scan and other exercises, individuals with chronic pain and others report feeling less pain, stress, anxiety, and depression.[4]

Like the body scan exercise, spot the success is meant to help redistribute attention so that we are less likely to succumb to the habit of only noticing what isn't going well. One student reflected, "Because I rarely deal with my feelings, good or bad, the good stuff tends to get lost and the negative emotions seem to be all I can feel. Writing out ten successes in the last twenty-four hours can be difficult at times, but it is very, very important for me, and it makes me feel better about myself."

Another way that spot the success can help balance your attention is its emphasis on events that occurred today rather than those completed in the past or tasks looming in the future. People are often self-critical when they worry about long-term projects or career prospects, and they may not register any of their daily accomplishments. Another student reflected, "As a person who obsesses about high standards and long-term goals, saying to myself 'Good job' for cleaning my apartment or eating dinner has been liberating. Acknowledging that each success, no matter how insignificant it may seem, is actually huge and worthy of praise has had a grounding effect on me."

Acknowledge Yourself Instead of Waiting for Others to Notice, Thank, Praise, or Reward You

Ruby's daily workload for her family was enormous. She prepared meals, cleaned, completed miscellaneous household tasks, and coordinated her kids' activities—in addition to working three days a week at a graphic design company. At times, Ruby's workload felt overwhelming. But she told me that what aggravated her the most was that her partner didn't seem to notice or appreciate how much she was doing. Her face was drawn as she spoke to me, and her posture was deflated, as though the lack of appreciation had sapped her energy.

Ruby's wish for her partner to acknowledge her work is an understandable one. People who feel gratitude from their partners do report higher levels of relationship satisfaction.[5] Ruby asked her partner to express more appreciation and gratitude for all that she did. Her partner agreed, but her partner's behavior didn't change much. In fact, it's common for members of cohabiting couples to underestimate the amount of housework that their partner contributes. If they're not there at the moment that their partner is completing tasks, it's harder to bring those tasks to mind.[6] So Ruby remained frustrated. While she still hoped that her partner could acknowledge her work more, what could she herself do to feel more appreciated and less depleted in the meantime?

I asked Ruby if she ever tried thanking *herself* for all that she was doing. I suggested that she really tune in to appreciate herself: the physical labor, the mental load that she carried, the endless coordination of tasks. What if she took a quick mental moment to really acknowledge and appreciate her completion of a task before moving on to the next thing? Would it be possible to even thank herself while she folded the laundry or cooked a meal? Is there any chance that some of that warmth, love, gratitude, and recognition that she craved from her partner could be found within herself? Although Ruby moved across the country before I could find out whether the strategy had helped her, I took my own advice, and I began to appreciate my own labor quite a bit more as I performed it, especially during the kinds of household and caregiving activities that are often invisible to others. Even though this skill doesn't fix the deeper systemic issues involved—the extent to which unpaid work is often ignored and undervalued, or unequally distributed among cohabiting adults—I appreciate that spotting household successes can improve my well-being.

What opportunities are there in your own life to give yourself credit for achievements that you typically wait for others to acknowledge? Perhaps you submitted an application, cleaned your home, or started exercising more regularly. Great! Well done! You might never hear from another person that these things matter; you may never receive any kind of external acknowledgment that you accomplished them. That's why it's so important to generate some sort of positive feedback within yourself in order to sustain and reinforce your good efforts.

It's easy to prioritize efforts that get rewarded by other people or with money. Paid work can seem more legitimate and important than unpaid work, because with paid work, people usually notice what you are doing, and, of course, you get money for doing it. Even people whose financial needs are met often find themselves increasing their amount of paid work and find it hard to do unpaid tasks. It's understandable to prioritize work that others see, but a lack of acknowledgment or praise, even from yourself, in other areas in life may compromise your health and well-being.

For instance, most people don't get paid for exercising. Many people feel disciplined in their work lives and truly want to take better care of their health, but they struggle to find the same kind of discipline when it comes to taking care of their own bodies. Finding an internal source of recognition, through spot the success or otherwise, can help.

Finding Nonobvious Success

Small, clear, task-based successes are an excellent way to begin to engage with spot the success. Start with the obvious: you took the vitamin, weeded the garden, sent the email, paid the bill, called your friend, or made the lasagna. During the past year, I've built up the habit of spotting the success when I empty the compost bin or take out the recycling and the trash. It doesn't actually feel like such a chore now, because I'm engaged in acknowledging the action as I'm doing it, and because I also savor a few breaths of fresh air. Plus, my practice of mentally rewarding myself for taking out the compost bin (and doing so repeatedly over time) has built up a positive feeling about doing it.

But let's take a moment to consider less obvious successes, as well as more complex ones. The other night, I left the dishes in the sink because I recognized that my body needed rest more than the dishes needed to be cleaned. That's a success as well—discerning the right amount of exertion versus rest—even though it might not seem like it, because the dishes remained undone. In another example, I had just finished picking up and putting the pieces of a crafting kit (beads, feathers, and assorted odds and ends) into its bag when my toddler turned the bag upside down and emptied its entire contents back onto the carpet, and I didn't get upset or angry. That success is tricky to notice because it reflects the absence of something (a frustrated outburst) rather than the presence of something (a tangible item that I accomplished). You might consider aspects of success hiding in what you consider to be failures or in unremarkable moments.

A poignant spot-the-success story comes from seventeenth-century Japan. The Zen master Tetsugen Doko (1630–1682) was an early leader of the Obaku school of Buddhism. Because the Buddhist sutras, important religious texts, were only available in Chinese at that time, Tetsugen decided to publish them in Japanese (about 70 percent of Japanese *kanji* characters and Chinese *hanzi* characters overlap, but because about 30 percent don't overlap, an accurate translation was needed). This endeavor would require an enormous amount of money to purchase and carve tens of thousands of wood-block plates. Over ten years, Tetsugen traveled the country to collect donations, small and large, toward his goal. He thanked every donor with sincere gratitude, regardless of the size of their donation. Finally, he amassed the funds needed to complete his goal.

But then the Uji River overflowed, ruining crops and supplies. Famine spread throughout the land. Instead of spending the money that he had collected to publish the sutras, Tetsugen used the money to save people from starvation. Then, he started over, traveling throughout the country in order to amass donations small and large (but mostly small). Several years later, an epidemic raged throughout the country. Again,

Tetsugen gave away what he had collected in order to help those in need. He then started his collecting for a third time. Twenty years later, Tetsugen had the money that he needed. In 1681, he supervised the creation of the first Japanese complete woodcut edition of the sutras. The printing blocks used for that first Japanese edition of the sutras can be viewed in the Obaku monastery in Kyoto. It is said that "Tetsugen made three sets of sutras, and that the first two invisible sets surpass even the last."[7]

What grips me the most about the story is its last sentence: the interpretation that Tetsugen's decision to redirect his fundraising to save lives is an action reflecting all of the beauty and wisdom of the Buddhist sutras—that his actions can even be viewed as sutras. A more commonplace response to the events would be to say, "Well, unfortunately, Tetsugen's goal of publishing the sutras was a frustrated and fragmented affair, and he failed twice before he succeeded." Instead, we can surmise that his success just looked different than he, or we, may have imagined. Saving lives both reflects and exceeds Tetsugen's original intention of improving people's lives by publishing the sutras.

Reframing Physical Labor as Exercise: The Curious Case of the Hotel Attendants

Cleaning hotel rooms is hard work, but is it exercise? Researchers asked eighty-four female room attendants, working in seven different hotels, whether they got regular exercise.[8] Two-thirds of the room attendants said that they did not exercise regularly, and 36.8 percent claimed that they never exercised. Next, the attendants were separated into two groups. Half of them were told that cleaning hotel rooms was good exercise and that it met the United States surgeon general's recommendations for physical activity. The other attendants weren't told anything.

Four weeks later, the women who had been told that their cleaning work was good exercise indicated that they thought of themselves as getting more exercise than they had before they heard about the physical benefits of their work. Measurements also showed that the attendants in the "informed" condition also had lost weight, reduced their body mass index, and lowered their blood pressure. Although their opinions had changed about whether or not cleaning hotel rooms counted as exercise, they did not report getting any more physical exercise outside of work hours.

How did perceiving their regular work as good exercise lead to actual physical health improvements for these room attendants? The answers aren't clear. It could reflect complex mind-body connections, in which viewing their work as exercise cascaded into positive physical results. Or, as authors Chip Heath and Dan Heath point out, thinking about their work as being actual physical exercise might have changed how they did their work.[9] Even though their workloads hadn't changed, the attendants who were told that their work was indeed exercise might have made the beds or vacuumed a little more vigorously—that is, they might have actually gotten more or better exercise even through doing the same work. But whatever change led to their improved health, it seemed to have begun with an "I'm already exercising" mindset.

Once you begin to regard various daily experiences in the light of success, you may be surprised by the way that a "success" framework can energize your behavior, reduce self-criticism, and improve your performance on work and other tasks. Even challenging mental states such as anxiety may have some features that you can channel to your advantage.

What Happens If You View Moderate Levels of Anxiety as Positive?

Standardized tests often provoke feelings of anxiety. You might imagine being about to take a high-pressure test, and then working yourself up into a mental loop. ("Gosh, I feel so anxious, I need to calm down—otherwise my anxiety will get the better of me and I will totally bomb this test!") In fact, in this example, anxiety itself is viewed as the threat to success. But what if you were to view anxiety as something that could actually help your performance rather than harm it?

At Harvard University, the researcher Jeremy Jamieson and his colleagues investigated whether influencing assumptions about exam-related anxiety could improve students' performance. The researchers recruited students who were preparing to take the Graduate Record Examination (GRE), a major exam necessary for admission to many graduate programs.[10] Next, they randomly divided the students in half before administering a practice GRE exam. Half of the students received no additional information, but the other half of the students read this information about anxious "arousal," here meant to reflect the feeling of being very alert and stimulated, right before the practice test:

> People think that feeling anxious while taking a standardized test will make them do poorly on the test. However, recent research suggests that arousal doesn't hurt performance on these tests and can even help performance . . . people who feel anxious during

a test might actually do better. This means that you shouldn't feel concerned if you do feel anxious while taking today's GRE test. [I]f you find yourself feeling anxious, simply remind yourself that your arousal could be helping you do well.[11]

The students who read the paragraph above performed better on the math section of their GRE practice test than the students who had not read it. When it came time to take the real test, the effect persisted. The same students (the ones who had read that anxious arousal could help performance) received significantly higher GRE math scores than did their peers on the actual exam. Just in case other factors might have influenced the different scores (for example, the amount of time students studied or their prior coursework), the researchers reanalyzed the data to account for those differences. Even after taking those other factors into account, the analyses demonstrated that being in the group of students who read about the benefits of arousal persisted in predicting significantly higher math GRE scores.

How did learning about the potential benefits of anxious arousal help students perform better? It's likely that students changed their minds about what their anxious arousal *meant*. Instead of assuming that their anxiety was a problem that would sabotage them, they could think of anxious arousal as normal and perhaps even helpful. Maybe that mindset made them less distracted by their anxiety and better able to focus on the material so that they could perform well on the test. Reading information about the potential benefits of anxiety can also boost students' confidence about their ability to cope with test-related stress.[12] In a similar set of studies, reframing anxiety as excitement, rather than trying to calm down, helped people to feel more excited and to perform better, whether the task involved public speaking, karaoke singing, or math.[13] Interestingly, the research shows that ignoring or suppressing stress does not seem to improve outcomes. Instead, learning that stressful feelings could be helpful (that is, reappraising what the stress actually means) has been demonstrated to benefit people more than ignoring, suppressing, or even accepting difficult feelings.[14]

What Are Appraisals and Reappraisals?

An appraisal is an interpretation of what something means. An appraisal might feel very "true," and of course, it *is* true in the sense that it is a thought that is truly happening. But appraisals are often not based in fact. They reflect assumptions and habits. I might assume that a colleague didn't think that the email I sent was important enough to merit a response. In reality, my colleague's own personal, work, or technological issues may have gotten in the way.

Appraisals turn out to be wildly important for mental health. A large part of our mental activity consists of assigning meaning to what happens. Even though we don't usually choose our appraisals on purpose, they form the link between what happens and how we feel. A habit of appraising events as meaning that there's something wrong with you (or that things around you will go wrong) usually leads to feelings of depression and/or anxiety. However, you can learn to observe appraisals and to reappraise how you're interpreting the meaning of circumstances and events. By using spot the success or related techniques, you can train yourself to appraise your actions, feelings, and circumstances in a way that is helpful and encouraging, and that enhances your mental health.

On a recent meditation retreat, I was assigned a room quite near the kitchen—perhaps about fifteen feet away from the dishwashing area. Even if I closed the door to my room, the kitchen noise remained very loud. Now, part of the work of being on a meditation retreat is to notice your interpretations (appraisals) of what's happening and to try out different, less judgmental ways of relating to your experiences. The loud kitchen noise presented an opportunity to practice different ways of mentally relating to my experience. But what method of relating should I use? Which one would help me have the best (or least annoyed) mood?

I could listen to the clanking and dinging sounds as simple sounds, through what Buddhists refer to as the "sense doors" of hearing. That is, I would focus more on the quality of the sound than on my own reactions to it. Or, I could notice my thoughts and feelings about the sounds, as well as related sensations in my body and mind (such as having tense shoulders or holding my breath). Those sorts of approaches reflect a sense of trying to accept my own sensations and feelings, and to work with them after they appear.

I tried both approaches. I paid attention to the sounds as sounds. ("There's a ding, I'm noticing its pitch and when it fades away; next, a loud clanking sound.") I observed some of the thoughts I was having: "I wish the noise would stop, or that it would become less loud. I wish I had a quieter room." I scanned my body for tightness or tension, and I noticed some feeling of knots in my neck and discomfort in my chest. My intention was to notice my thoughts and feelings in a nonjudgmental way and to sort of let them be. After a few instances of practicing in this way, I felt sort of peaceful and sort of bothered at the same time. Basically, I felt a bit more relaxed about my own discomfort.

But then, a thought popped into my head: "Someone is doing the dishes, and it isn't me." In my everyday, non-retreat life, I do the vast majority of the dishes for five people—three meals a day plus snacks—for what seems like hours every day. But on retreat, my work assignment was cooking, not dishes. During those moments in my room on retreat, as the loud kitchen noises went on, I could sit back and appreciate that other people were washing the dishes. A wave of relief swept over me, dissolving my body's tension. Instead of annoyance, I felt gratitude. The same sounds that had provoked feelings of annoyance suddenly yielded actual joy. I smiled. I was stunned by the power of the new appraisal to generate entirely different feelings. The sounds of the dishes never bothered me again over the remaining six days of the retreat. With my reappraisal ("Someone is doing the dishes, and it's not me"), the sounds continued to elicit feelings of gratitude, happiness, and relaxation.

The experience that a reappraisal approach was more effective than trying to accept my feelings matches the outcomes of research studies comparing both techniques. Philippe Goldin, a neuroscientist and professor at the University of California, Davis, and his colleagues explain that reappraisal works better than acceptance in reducing negative feelings, and that it also involves using more of the brain's resources.[15] Another important aspect of reappraisal is that it's a form of "antecedent-focused coping" rather than "response-focused coping."[16] That is, reappraisal works by changing the precursor (the thought) that leads to emotional and physical responses. In contrast, emotion regulation strategies of acceptance or suppression only start after difficult feelings have already developed. It's understandably more effective to intervene *before* challenging emotions and sensations arise than after they're already there. However, it's also possible that the longer-term effects of cultivating acceptance and nonjudgment toward your experiences might themselves contribute to antecedent-focused coping. If those tendencies are already in place before a challenging event occurs, they might help you feel calmer when you suddenly realize that you will need to wait twenty minutes in line or postpone your plans because of a flat tire.

Spot the success is all about influencing your appraisals, because it encourages you to appreciate both small and large behaviors through the lens of success. The practice can help you view your normal activities as meaningful, doable, aligned with your values, and as making a positive contribution. One student noted that "I use spot the success whenever I'm overwhelmed or stressed because it makes me perceive the rest of the day in a more positive light. After I make the list, I find it easier to finish the rest of my tasks because my stress levels have gone down."

Spot the Success and Mindfulness Perspectives on Nonjudgment

Does spot the success clash with core mindfulness perspectives? Spot the success does seem rather different from practicing mindful nonjudgment, in which you try to notice experiences without judging them or interpreting what they might mean about you (see chapter 3). It's true that there is a bit of judgment involved in labeling something a "success." But the evaluative part of the exercise is meant to stop there. Spot the success isn't about assessing how well you did something; it only means noticing that something helpful occurred (or that you were able to refrain from doing something).

Both spot the success and mindfulness practice bring attention to small experiences, ones that we often take for granted or that simply get lost in the rush of life. Practicing mindfulness, both in terms of formal meditation and in everyday life, can complement spot the success. What happens if we show up to those moments differently, with more awareness and appreciation? One student wrote that practicing spot the success "makes me more mindful of these acts while I'm in the process of doing them."

Practicing the skill of reappraisal is a core component of both spot the success and many mindfulness techniques. Viewing experiences through the lens of moment-to-moment sensations, without judging them or ruminating about them, involves considering stimuli in a new way. The idea of "de-centering," or experiencing moments as a nonjudging witness instead of being overly identified with emotions and related stories, can also be seen as a type of intentional reappraisal. Similarly, using mindfulness practices to cultivate compassion and good wishes involves choosing a particular mental approach that might differ from the default way that you treat yourself or others.

Another part of mindfulness practice involves building awareness for the interconnectedness of people, actions, and the earth. That appreciation is present, for instance, in the mindfulness practice of cultivating good wishes toward all beings. As you practice spot the success, noticing that you wrote a condolence card to a friend, made a health appointment, or that you put a banana peel into the compost bin can boost feelings of connection—these small, everyday actions can be reappraised as helpful steps that you've taken to tend a relationship, or to care for your body or the planet.

The Role of Cognitive Reappraisal
in Trauma and Mental Health

Experiencing painful events, situations, and feelings takes a toll on mental health. In addition to the pain of the trauma itself, many people criticize themselves for their trauma-related feelings. That self-criticism often takes the form of negative "trauma appraisals" about themselves. It's common to blame oneself for the trauma ("If only I had done X, Y, or Z, it wouldn't have happened"), or to view oneself as defective for feeling traumatized, anxious, and depressed. Common appraisals after trauma include thoughts related to shame, self-blame, anger, betrayal, fear, esteem, safety, trust, power, control, intimacy, and alienation (feeling disconnected from other people).[17] Because trauma-related appraisals, including self-criticism, so strongly color our feelings after trauma, revising those appraisals—either by normalizing common responses to trauma or by acknowledging successful steps toward healing—can make it easier to cope.

Negative appraisals about trauma are linked with higher levels of stress and depression.[18] One study investigated firefighters' tendencies to form negative appraisals about themselves during their training period. Firefighters' pre-trauma appraisals turned out to predict the severity of PTSD (post-traumatic stress disorder) symptoms that they developed after experiencing trauma within the four-year follow-up period.[19] In fact, people's appraisals about their traumatic experiences—that is, interpretations about what trauma means—contribute to mental health symptoms over and above the amount of trauma that people have experienced.[20]

As a clinical psychologist, my work involves challenging patients' self-critical trauma appraisals and encouraging reappraisals. For instance, difficult feelings after stress and trauma are normal, not a sign that there's something wrong with a person. In fact, it's the sign of a working emotional system to respond to trauma by being very alert or anxious, or by avoiding similar situations. However, feelings and behaviors that are adaptive during the trauma can cause suffering if they persist. A spot-the-success framework with trauma can help people appreciate, rather than criticize, normal responses to trauma. And it can also help people along the way as they try to practice and reinforce new behaviors.

Spotting the success with trauma involves reframing normal emotional responses like anxiety or withdrawing as being potentially helpful at the time of trauma or just afterward. For instance, a person who is assaulted by an acquaintance at a party might then refrain from socializing with new people or attending events, or they might start monitoring every interaction for signs of danger, in order to protect themselves from further harm. Those behaviors might be part of what the person needs to help feel safe and to recover, but eventually they might cause more difficulties, such as loneliness or social anxiety. Then, after some period of establishing a sense of safety and coping with trauma-related distress, the same person might benefit from developing new behaviors, like having a short conversation at the supermarket or accepting an invitation rather than declining it. During the process of healing from serious trauma, it's important to spot the successes along the way, in order to keep them going and to build upon them.

Given how important appraisals are, how do you go about

changing them? There's a risk in being overly simplistic—that is, in telling yourself or another person to simply have different thoughts so that they'll feel differently. Just deciding to think about something differently doesn't seem to do the trick. One approach, cognitive processing therapy, involves first identifying mental "stuck points" after trauma (as often appraisals lurk below conscious awareness) and then proceeds to challenge them over a three-month period.[21]

For instance, if the appraisal after trauma is "I can never trust anyone again after what happened to me," a person might consider whether they needed to have complete trust in a person in order to be friendly with them, or if some people seem more trustworthy than others. If the appraisal is "I need to be on guard all of the time," a person could investigate whether being on edge is beneficial in every situation or if some situations seemed to require more vigilance than others. Patients also investigate the function of the stuck point. How does having this belief affect your life? If you didn't have that belief, what would happen?

With long-standing appraisals, it's unlikely that trying out a new appraisal would make someone feel better right away. Cognitive processing therapy (CPT) usually spans twelve weeks, and it involves working with a therapist who provides emotional support and guidance. The evidence does indicate that the approach works well for many survivors of trauma.[22] And in fact, the process of changing appraisals is a key mechanism that explains *why* CPT works.[23] Practicing cognitive appraisal can also help people cope with chronic illnesses such as HIV,[24] and is associated with lower levels of depression.[25]

Variations on Spot the Success: Done Lists, Reality-Based Self-Congratulation, and Gratitude Lists

Several years after I started teaching spot the success in my psychology courses and describing the technique in psychotherapy sessions with my patients, I learned that the practice was also referred to as a "done list." In most ways, they are the same. They emphasize something positive that you contributed to that has already occurred. In that way, either title conveys that the list is the opposite of a to-do list. In fact, Marc Andreessen, cofounder of Netscape, calls the practice an "anti-to-do list." He encourages people to write down "every time you do something—anything—useful during the day" on a three-by-five index card and then to look at the card at the end of the day to "marvel" at their successes. Within a work context, such "successes" might be easier to identify. But what about—as mentioned above—successes outside of paid work, such as caregiving?

Andrea Dekker is a mom who runs a website with organizing tips, recipes, and other tools. She explained that "I can easily feel defeated and down in the dumps if I get to the end of my day with several to-dos left undone. Looking back, my to-do lists were much too ambitious for a mother of an infant who never slept, but never-the-less, I constantly struggled with feelings of inadequacy, inefficiency, and a very negative self-worth." She shares the following "done list," for a particular day:

- made the bed
- took a shower
- made dinner

- held Nora while she took a nap
- walked around the block
- kept a newborn alive (with basically zero parenting experience!)
- kept food in the fridge
- did a load of laundry
- read 5 pages in my book
- picked up the living room
- made breakfast and dinner for our family (and the international students that lived with us at the time)
- packed lunches
- held a fussy baby for a vast majority of the day[26]

As I look over the list above, I'm struck by the amount of physical energy and persistence necessary to complete most of the tasks. Holding a fussy baby all day long while trying to get other things done takes both physical and mental stamina. Because it's so hard to get anything else done while taking care of an infant, it can often seem like you haven't done anything, when really you've been providing an intense level of care all day long. Feeling isolated and overwhelmed while taking care of small kids can be exacerbated by a larger culture that devalues that work. New parents often feel distressed, which can be exacerbated by a lack of emotional and financial support. It can seem impossible to meet their own and others' expectations, despite their best efforts.

For Andrea, making a conscious decision to acknowledge those efforts paid off. She reflected that "honestly, making a done list is one of the simplest things I do to instantly boost my mood." You can choose whether you prefer the language of "spot the success" or a "done list." In either case, I encourage challenging yourself to find nonobvious successes, including those that you might not consider to be completed actions, such as not losing your temper with a family member, or having a flash of creativity that hasn't yet led to anything tangible.

REALITY-BASED SELF-CONGRATULATION

Dr. Joel Almeida is a writer, doctor, and mentor to other physicians who describes an exercise that is quite similar to spot the success. He calls his technique "reality-based self-congratulation," or REBS. Dr. Almeida encourages people to reinforce every small step in the right direction toward their goals with an immediate phrase conveying self-congratulation. REBS can accelerate progress toward your goals, and it can also help train your mind away from self-criticism, perfectionism, or comparisons between yourself and others. The phrase could be quite short, such as "I did this" or "I did it, I'm okay."

Dr. Almeida shared that at one time he was struggling to lose weight, even though he exercised regularly. He was placed on statin medications for high cholesterol. He saw an opportunity to use REBS for each nutritious meal that he ate, each half hour that he refrained from grazing on snacks, and every time he got back on track after a setback. He describes REBS as "a steady stream of self-congratulation that is based on real advances" that led him to permanently lose several inches around his waist, to no longer need the statin medications for high cholesterol, and to feel more peaceful and clearheaded.

My students also report benefiting emotionally from congratulating themselves for small steps toward their goals. One student observed that "praising myself for small victories such as cleaning my room, being on time, and getting in the gym has made me appreciate myself more. I am generally happier and more energetic about life because I feel good about myself."

GRATITUDE LISTS

Spot the success and gratitude lists each involve purposefully looking at your situation in a different way. To create a gratitude list, you would identify things, people, and circumstances about which you feel appreciation or gratitude. The appreciation evoked by practicing spot the success or by writing gratitude lists involves both thoughts and emotions. When you appreciate something or someone, you acknowledge its meaning, and you also experience a positive emotional association with it.[27] In research involving 243 participants, appreciation played a significant role in life satisfaction, even after controlling for personality differences.[28]

Spot the success and gratitude lists reflect specific kinds of appreciation. Whereas a gratitude list usually focuses on external circumstances (external "things" or conditions to be grateful for), spot the success involves generating appreciation for your own contributions. And an important reason to focus on this type of appreciation is to counteract self-critical tendencies. If you struggle to acknowledge what you're doing well, spot the success is designed to help you do that. Noticing your own helpful actions can shift how you see yourself and how you treat yourself.

Once it becomes more of a lived experience, you might notice some of the barriers between spot the success and gratitude lists begin to dissolve a little bit. You can be grateful to have a home, even as you appreciate yourself for cleaning it. Maybe you even feel both of those things within the same moment of cleaning. You might notice the "I" dissolve a bit, so that you're left with appreciation and gratitude—not so much about yourself or about external circumstances but about the presence of so many gifts and interconnections of which you are a part.

The writer Celeste Murphy observed that after a triumph in her career, "I was filled with gratitude. And gratitude allowed me to sing praises, not for my own awesomeness alone, but for everyone who assisted in helping me reach my goal." She noted that no one accomplishes anything without other people involved, and that, "my small achievement strengthened my connection in the world."[29] Murphy's description conveys how you can mindfully acknowledge your own actions as well as the help that other people provided.

You can also try out both practices (spot the success and gratitude lists), and then notice what happens. Many people report benefits from intentionally practicing gratitude, but other people notice that they feel worse. The writer Liz Brown observed that keeping gratitude lists caused her to feel ashamed about her feelings. Her gratitude lists led to more negative self-talk as she saw herself as self-pitying or ungrateful ("My life isn't so bad. What's wrong with me?"), and she only felt better when she genuinely acknowledged her painful emotions and experiences.[30] Take care that you're not suppressing difficult feelings when you practice either spot the success or when you write a gratitude list. Neither exercise is meant to cover up or suppress deeper levels of pain but rather to help balance attention away from self-criticism or a mental pattern of only noticing what isn't going well. Emotional pain can indeed benefit from attention and care (see chapter 6, "Allowing All Feelings, Skillfully").

"Spot the Success" versus "Looking on the Bright Side"

Is spot the success the same as looking on the bright side? It depends what you mean by "looking on the bright side." Both spot the success and the idea of looking on the bright side do involve considering a more positive perspective. However, the advice to "look on the bright side" can sometimes convey criticism toward a person's thoughts or feelings. "Look on the bright side" might imply that people should suppress difficult perspectives, or that they should cover up difficult feelings by pretending that all is well.

Cognitive reappraisal practices seem to work best when combined with higher levels of emotional awareness.[31] That means that knowing how you really feel across your full range of emotions seems to be helpful when trying out new approaches to manage your thoughts and feelings. This exercise isn't about covering up what is painful or difficult by forcing yourself to view everything as positive.

In fact, suppressing emotions isn't a very effective strategy for regulating mood.[32] Suppressing feelings can even worsen depression.[33] When researchers observe what happens when people are told to suppress their feelings—including the example above about test anxiety, or other research where folks were instructed to give short speeches[34]—people don't perform better by suppressing their feelings. However, when they reappraise their experiences (interpret them in a different way), people's performances improve.

Spot the success is more like shining a light on forgotten areas of experience (successes) than it is relegating problems to the darkness. You can think of the exercise as expanding your awareness rather than contracting it. The exercise is meant to help balance out tendencies toward excessive self-criticism by opening up other ways of looking at your day.

If you find yourself struggling with the exercise, you can remember that it's often challenging to try out a new approach. When you're practicing spot the success, please don't berate yourself for any criticism, minimizing accomplishments, self-doubt, or other negative thoughts that arise. Instead, the idea is to make room for a new and encouraging perspective and to actually *practice* inhabiting that new perspective, over and over again.

REFLECTION QUESTIONS

1. Do you make lists? If so, what's the best part of making a list? Have you ever written something down on a list that you've already done, just to acknowledge that you did it?
2. What "successes" in your daily life seem more obvious, and which "successes" are less obvious?
3. How often do you tell yourself to "look on the bright side" or to "count your blessings"? Does it work or help you to do that, or does it make you feel worse about yourself?
4. Do you tend to discount your own achievements? Can you notice when this is happening, and can you experiment with inviting a sense of accomplishment?
5. In what way do your daily tasks align with your deepest values?
6. If you practiced spot the success, how did you feel afterward?

3

Nonjudgment, or at Least a Lot Less Judgment

IN MEDITATION WORKSHOPS and retreats, a common theme is to develop the skill of observing experiences without judging them. Instructors advise attendees to notice through the "sense doors" of one's eyes, ears, mouth, and bodily movements—pre-verbally, if you can. Is it possible to really tune in to the texture and flavors of the food that you're tasting, even before you label it "good" or "bad"? Can you take in the sound of a bird chirping, perhaps even before your mind steps in with the word *bird*? You might find it quite difficult to notice experiences without automatically judging them. However, the process of trying to register sensations first, even before interpretations and judgments emerge, can help shift old patterns. The effort itself can make a difference in how you react to what's going on, both within yourself and in response to the outside world.

During one meditation workshop I attended several years ago, the session leader had worked with us for most of the day, encouraging us with meditation sessions in which we practiced noticing thoughts, feelings, and other experiences without judgment. Then, we had a break. At meditation events, you're often encouraged to treat everything as a meditation, even on breaks: rising to get up from your meditation cushion, eating lunch, going to the bathroom, putting on your coat, and so on. The idea is to observe—as much as possible—all of your actions and experiences with a quality of calm, kind noticing rather than through the lens of judgment ("I like this; I don't like that"). With that intention, my friend Brighid and I went to get some tea and began a walk together. I continued the mental effort of noticing with interest and curiosity while trying to set aside the automatic tendency to judge anything as good or bad. I was walking outside with that mindset—in fact, consciously cultivating that mindset—when something fell down from the sky and into my open cup of tea. A bird had pooped *right in my cup*.

Aside from the precision of the bird's hit, the weirdest part was that I wasn't upset. I kept up the intention and practice of noticing with openness as we headed back to the refreshment table, where I got a new cup of tea. In almost any other situation, with a different mindset, I might have leapt to judgment. ("Ew! This is terrible! Just my luck.") But in this case, my consciously cultivated mindset influenced my reaction, and I found the situation quite funny.

The word *meditation* can evoke a range of responses. Perhaps you're quite familiar with meditation practice, or perhaps you find the idea unappealing or foreign. In either case, I recommend meditation as an effective method for reducing self-criticism and other automatic judgments. When people first start to meditate, they often notice self-criticism about meditation practice itself ("I'm bad at this"). If you can tolerate or even expect that meditation might not feel easy at first, it can provide an excellent vehicle for decreasing self-criticism. Meditation allows you to practice handling self-criticism in the moment that it arises. It involves redirecting the mind away from self-criticism, over and over, with the effect that self-criticism can decrease and become much less habitual.

As noted in the introduction, *mindfulness* reflects paying attention to your experiences in the present moment on purpose, and without judging them. Mindfulness can occur either during certain moments where you're focusing on trying to be mindful, or during your daily activities when you bring a quality of present-moment attention to them. *Meditation*, on the other hand, refers to a specific time that you've set aside to practice a particular method or technique. For instance, a meditation session might involve sitting down on a pillow and trying to notice your breath for twenty minutes at a time.

Although people describe benefits from a range of different mindfulness practices, the evidence indicates that practicing more consistently and for a greater number of minutes at a time are both associated with increased benefits.[1] A committed practice eliminates the risk of carrying a general idea of cultivating mindfulness without really checking on whether or how much you're doing it. Becoming more mindful of your experiences will happen naturally as a result of regular meditation practice.

Meditation can be a helpful strategy for self-criticism because it involves repeatedly building another way to relate to yourself besides self-criticism. Often, the pull of self-criticism is just too strong to address head-on. Many of us have had a great deal of practice with self-criticism. We've built our self-criticism up quite strongly over the years, even if that self-criticism has been unconscious or involuntary. In your mind, self-criticism has built foundations, tunnels, skyscrapers, and (this last part is real, not a metaphor) interconnected and efficient networks. We absorb input from our families, peers, and cultures of origin, and then perpetuate the same judgments about how we should be, what we should do, what we should look like. People also learn to criticize themselves from witnessing their parents' self-criticism, or from criticism within adult relationships. In Neal Stephenson's novel *Fall*, the main character's self-criticism stems from his combined, internalized ex-girlfriends, who "lived on between his ears immortally, speaking to him at the strangest times, actually changing the way he thought and behaved," with "a few choice remarks that would make him feel bad."[2]

Instead of focusing on self-criticism in particular, meditation reduces self-criticism by decreasing judgmental tendencies in general. There are places and times for rapid judgments—if you're a firefighter, soccer player, or emergency medical technician, for instance, it's a pretty important skill to have. However, automatic judgments often have elements of beating yourself up, restricting what parts of yourself or life are acceptable, reflecting stereotyping and other biases, or trying to control everything. A mind characterized by rapid, automatic judgments is vulnerable not only to misery but also to stereotyping, racism, and other biases. The world becomes narrow, contracted. We pick what we like, what we're good at, what interests us, and then reject everything else. And we reject parts of ourselves, or label them unacceptable, and that rejection can hurt. The alternative is to consciously cultivate the skill of noticing experiences without judging them.

Meditation strengthens the "witness" part of you, the nonjudgmental or kind observer, while allowing the "judging" part of yourself to settle down or to become just another thought or feeling to observe among many. One student wrote this description of joining with the "observer" self during meditation:

> Sometimes when I meditate, it feels like I am rising to a higher version of myself, floating above the clouds of my own thoughts to join with a more stable and noble self who is always watching. I feel that when I meditate, I connect with that observer self, who has endless compassion for my own thoughts, feelings, and behavior. Spending time with this "self" has made me a stronger person because those qualities shine through in my daily life; I am more stable, more able to detach from unhelpful thoughts, and can do all of this while being a little more compassionate and loving toward myself.

In this way, meditation promotes awareness of your feelings without judging them, a capacity that significantly predicts happiness, even after accounting for personality differences.[3] Another student observed that "my ability to recognize and regulate my own emotions was heightened and streamlined after a couple of weeks of meditation practice."

Although many beginning meditators expect themselves to feel peaceful during meditation or to "clear the mind," practicing meditation involves mental challenges such as distraction, boredom, doubt, sleepiness, and even self-criticism. The practice of noticing feelings and behaviors without judging them, over and over again, is a path toward less self-criticism and less judgment in general. As one student put it, observing without judging "has manifested in my life outside of meditating. I find myself being kinder to myself and withholding self-criticism."

In research studies investigating whether meditation and other mindfulness practices help people with depression, anxiety, or post-traumatic stress, investigators have identified reducing judgment as a key mechanism of action—a major ingredient that explains *why* mindfulness improves mental health.[4] Meditation helps people "suspend or disrupt negative or self-critical appraisal."[5] Because reducing judgment doesn't seem to happen by just deciding, you have to practice a new way until it becomes as strong as the old way.

Core Exercise

To practice mindful nonjudgment, find a seated posture that feels comfortable, dignified, and relaxed. Set an intention to try hard to focus the sensation of your breathing (wherever you feel the breath most strongly in your body), but not so much so that you feel stressed about it. Remember that your task is to notice that your mind wandered, to try to refrain from judging yourself for that experience, and then to return your focus to the breath, over and over. Even if you do it a hundred times in five minutes, each time you return your focus nonjudgmentally offers a valuable antidote to self-judgment.

Put succinctly, the exercise is to pay attention to your breathing, but when your mind wanders, bring it back without judging it. If judgment arises, bring your attention back to your breath, just as you would if any other thought arises during your meditation practice.

Sounds straightforward, right? However, when you sit down to meditate, your mind usually goes crazy. It flies everywhere—to the conversation you had this morning or the email that you plan to write after lunch. But that moment of frustration ("Ugh! There my mind goes again!") and self-judgment ("Why can't I do this right?") is exactly the target of practice for mindful nonjudgment. Noticing this pattern during mindfulness practice—and consciously trying to observe it without judgment—is the gold in your pan, not the dirt. You may have to remind yourself that practicing not judging yourself for mind wandering (that is, noticing it but refraining from judging) is your complete goal with this practice—not keeping your mind locked onto your breathing.

In my experience, the biggest frustration for beginning meditators is self-judgment.

It will take effort not to judge yourself. It's hard not to judge yourself as you try to focus on your breathing, not to judge yourself for where it goes ("I can't believe I'm rehashing that same argument with my boyfriend *again*"), and not to judge yourself for how many times you have to bring your mind back to your breathing during a practice session. People with ADHD sometimes find that refraining from self-judgment about becoming distracted is especially difficult, but if they can tolerate the initial self-judgment and keep meditating, the evidence shows that meditation practice can improve ADHD symptoms and overall well-being.[6] Practicing being less judgmental about mind-wandering (that is, about the mindfulness practice itself) seems to generalize very well into making people less self-critical, less anxious, and less depressed in everyday life.

Research studies pinpoint where the action of meditation practice actually is: noticing where your mind went and returning it to this moment, again and again, without judging yourself for having lost focus. One group of meditation researchers divided participants into groups who received different instructions. One group was told to monitor their attention, that is, to simply observe where their minds went. Another group was instructed to notice where their minds went but to then practice self-acceptance (noticing where your mind went, and then accepting how and where it wandered in a nonjudgmental way). After analyzing the data, the researchers determined that the latter group developed greater abilities to manage their own attention.[7]

I work with many college students who are just beginning to meditate or practice other forms of mindfulness. Practicing meditation requires hard work, because it involves changing long-standing patterns of attention and concentration. Students often describe overwhelming self-criticism during meditation—in particular, their self-judgment about becoming distracted. I work very hard to convince each student that this is normal and that learning to handle both the distractions and the self-judgment is valuable. Here is one student's account of the way that mindfulness worked to first illuminate and then reduce self-criticism:

> Toward the beginning of my mindfulness practice, I would get upset with myself for not being able to focus on my breathing for a long period of time, which would lead to more self-deprecating thoughts. But as I have practiced mindfulness more, I have learned to treat the times when my mind wanders as not bad things, but simply just as things that occur. I have tried to bring this into more of my everyday thinking.

It has definitely helped me talk and think to myself in a nicer and more understanding way.

This chapter emphasizes seated breath meditation (also called sitting meditation, breathing meditation, and various other names in different contexts and spiritual traditions), but there are many other ways to meditate. Among other well-known approaches are counting ten breaths and then starting over; paying attention to the sounds that you hear in this moment; walking meditation, in which you focus on the bodily motion of the walking process; and the body scan meditation, where you mentally scan the sensations of your body from head to toe. In each case, the idea is to focus on what's happening in the present moment and to bring your mind back when it wanders. This chapter emphasizes seated breath meditation because that form of meditation is especially helpful for reducing judgment.[8]

Methods of Returning Your Focus without Judging Yourself

It can be difficult to refrain from self-judgment when you become distracted during meditation. Instead of just trying not to judge yourself, you might try out one of these methods of returning your focus to your breath:

- With enthusiasm, like you're having a party. I use this with myself when one part of my mind is focused on my breathing, but another part is thinking about other things. When I notice my attention is divided, I imagine gathering all of the parts of my attention together and celebrating that reunited quality of attention as I approach the next breath: "We're all here for breath number seven, Hooray!"

- With humor. As a TV anchor on *Weekend Update*: "Aaaaaaand we're back."
- As a curious detective, noticing the sensations of your attention departing and returning.
- With appreciation for your efforts or for your intention.
- With a warm welcome, "Welcome home!"
- With normalizing, "Yup, that's what minds do."
- With understanding toward self-criticism. If self-criticism occurs, notice the criticism itself without judging it.
- With "noting" that your attention has wandered, perhaps with a short label about where it went ("ex-girlfriend," "thinking," "work," or "planning"). Some people use the word "thinking" to note any of these categories before returning to the breath.
- If you observed yourself judging, then with the song, "Here comes the judge!"
- With compassionate understanding ("For sure, it's challenging to meditate and to maintain focus when you are tired/hungry/crying/hearing your neighbors arguing").

Any of these techniques can be a touchstone for noticing and handling distractions during meditation. You might identify one strategy that seems particularly helpful for you, and then plan to implement it during your next meditation session. For instance, one of my students wrote, "I find I will be meditating and my mind is being bombarded with thoughts. I have found the noting technique to be something that is very helpful because it focuses on recognizing the distractions, letting them go and then redirecting my focus back."

Handling Projected Judgment

It's normal to want to be liked and to want people to think well of you. The thought "What will people think of me?" can facilitate making friends, creating positive experiences in the workplace, and generally contributing to a well-functioning society. But the thought can get out of hand. We don't just judge ourselves and judge other people. We also project our judgment of ourselves onto others, so that we live in the space of imagining what others think of us. It's a powerful mental force, and it arises in the guises of status, saving face, hiding vulnerability, serving the ego and superego, and even earning a living if your job involves others' views of you.

Students at my university's counseling center often reported extreme agitation from always worrying about what other people were thinking about them. Several students proclaimed very clearly: "I hate meeting new people." The word "hate" seemed to reflect the fear of what others would think of them—a fear so intense that it was more like agony.

In high school, I remember constantly worrying that my peers were judging my looks and my clothes—in part because I would hear them comment about others' looks and clothes on a daily basis. As a singer, I loved creating music with different groups of musicians, but their conversations also reflected how *well* each person was singing. Being constantly evaluated is baked into our society—through grades at school, job applications, and needing to please work supervisors. Or even just by walking down the street. In circumstances of abuse or racism, being very attuned to how others are thinking of you is actually adaptive, even though that attunement can be a painful mental place to inhabit, and the fear of others' thoughts about you can persist beyond the circumstances that require it.

And then there's gender. Female people are usually conditioned to see themselves through others' eyes, and to imagine how others are gauging our level of attractiveness and the ways that we stand, speak, walk, or act. The author Lily King writes, "You get trained early on as a woman to perceive how others are perceiving you, at the great expense of what you yourself are feeling about them. Sometimes you mix the two up in a terrible tangle that's hard to unravel."[9] The identity of being female can get so wrapped up with roles of caregiving, entertaining, attracting, or pleasing other people. Moving away from always attending to others' thoughts about us can feel strange at first, but it gets easier with practice. Specific mindfulness techniques, such as focusing on the sensations of the breath, can train the mind to focus on present-moment lived experience rather than on imagining others' thoughts about you.

Male gender norms also contain difficult challenges. Men often grow up learning that they should seem tough and in control, and that they should refrain from experiencing or displaying a full range of emotions. Males may consciously or even unconsciously criticize themselves for having emotions such as sadness, anxiety, uncertainty, and tenderness—that is, experiences beyond those that they learned to view as acceptable. Interestingly, many workplaces now require men to demonstrate "soft skills" that might include admitting mistakes, showing awareness of one's own emotional strengths and vulnerabilities, encouraging coworkers effectively, sharing joy in others' successes, and managing others' feelings in a sensitive and responsive manner.[10] One way that male-socialized people can benefit from mindfulness practices is by practicing the skill of noticing a wider range of feelings and sensations than those reflected in traditional gender norms.[11]

For instance, one of my students reflected that his default response to himself whenever he felt upset was "MAN UP!" It didn't matter if he felt nervous, angry, sick, or confused; the phrase "MAN UP!" would arise. As he began to explore this reaction, he observed that underneath the phrase lurked a fear of disappointing himself or letting his family down. Over the span of a four-week course that included meditation practice, he found that he was able to begin noticing his feelings without judging them and without worrying about others' opinions about him quite as much. He wrote, "I've started to slowly like myself, and to take care of my mental health."

How Meditation Breaks Up Our Default Thought Patterns

Mental habits such as self-criticism reflect established physical brain networks, built up over the years. Changing up those networks—both their physical structures and the ways that they operate—requires us to repeatedly practice new patterns.

You can visualize brain networks like a city map that changes over time: the roads get bigger and stronger the more you use them. Creating a new road takes much more energy than zipping along your usual route. This metaphor can help you picture what's happening in the brain when neuroscientists say, "Neurons that fire together wire together." That is, the more a group of neurons communicates with other neurons in a particular way, the more they physically build up those "roads," or networks, connecting different parts of the brain.

Brain activity involves two specific networks: the task positive network (TPN) and the default mode network (DMN)—the latter of which we looked at in chapter 1. When one network is active, the other network is much less active, and vice versa. A third network, the salience network, is involved in switching between the two.

The task positive network (TPN) dominates when you are paying attention to something in the present moment. If you're engaged in your work, playing sports, making music, or pursuing another task in a focused way, TPN activity is prominent. Brain regions involved in the TPN include the lateral prefrontal cortex, the anterior cingulate cortex, the insula, and the somatosensory cortex.

When you're not doing much of anything, your brain is still quite busy. The DMN (including the medial prefrontal cortex, posterior cingulate cortex, inferior parietal lobule, and the hippocampal formation) is active—passing information along, modifying it, and processing it—in habitual ways such as rumination (thinking about the same things over and over again, especially memories and past experiences, without active problem-solving), self-referential thinking (thinking about yourself, in the usual ways that you do that), and judgment (deciding whether things are good, bad, or neutral).

The DMN isn't all bad, and we need it to survive. The DMN helps us connect the past, present, and future, and helps us maintain our identity and our understanding of the world. We couldn't really get along without it. We need to be able to predict what might be needed in an upcoming situation, and to remember people and other information. The neuroscientist Marcus Raichle asserts that the DMN provides integration that is necessary for survival.

The DMN is active as we make judgments. Raichle explains, "It's not only important to remember what's important, but also to put a value on what's important. The part of the default mode network up front, down almost between your eyes, just above your nose, has to do with deciding whether something is good, bad, or indifferent. In other words, input from our body and the external world passes through this area of the brain before continuing on to the amygdala and the hypothalamus and the brain stem, which produce the emotional responses we experience all the time in our daily lives—everything that has to do with us getting along in the world."[12]

Although the DMN appears to help with physical survival, its overuse seems to contribute to suffering. Rumination and self-judgment—prominent during DMN activity—are linked with depression, anxiety, and other mental health difficulties. In fact, more functional connectivity between DMN regions is related to a tendency to ruminate and to unhappiness.[13] In the DMN, many of us have a brain network that is working too much and too efficiently, in the sense that it is highly developed and quick to activate. That's because our mental habits have shaped the DMN's structure and function.

Because the DMN helps determine how experiences and thoughts relate to yourself ("What does this mean about me and about my life?"), it leads to what the mindfulness teacher Jon Kabat-Zinn calls "selfing," or interpreting life experience through the constant background narration of "I, me, mine" or "the story of me."[14] Kabat-Zinn advises that we need to consciously work to balance the tendency of "selfing" in order to have a peaceful mental life. And one way to do that balancing work is through meditation.

Research studies provide evidence that meditation reduces DMN activity.[15] It doesn't seem to matter what kinds of meditation people practice (for instance, techniques that focus on concentration or compassion); research studies demonstrate reduced DMN activity results regardless of the type of meditation practiced.[16] Overall, the brains of experienced meditators show less DMN activity and greater activity in other brain networks—and that holds true whether they are in the midst of meditation or not.[17] Meditation seems to enhance activity in the salience network, so that it's easier to switch out of the DMN when you catch yourself ruminating. Meditation practice builds connectivity between the brain's networks and the ability to switch between them,[18] leading to less "selfing," less rumination, less judgment, and to higher levels of well-being.[19]

You might consider how DMN and TPN operate within the moments of meditation. As you sit down and begin to pay attention to each breath in the present moment, that effort engages your task positive network (TPN). However, it's likely that your DMN will interrupt with its usual material ("I'm bad at this! Rumination of the Top 40 current worries and past mistakes! More 'selfing' and self-judgment!"). Your job is to notice that your attention has shifted away from the breath and then to return your attention. That process activates the salience network, quiets the DMN, and reengages the TPN.[20] The more you judge yourself during the process of noticing your distraction, the more DMN activity you are having. Judging yourself less and returning your mind to the breath more quickly means less DMN activity and more practice engaging the salience network and the TPN.

Over time, meditation builds the capacity to switch out of the DMN, to do so on purpose, and to have less overall activity in the DMN. Meditation practice enhances the connection between your brain's networks and your control over which network is activated.[21] This capacity generalizes beyond your meditation practice and into everyday life. In fact, over time, meditation practice reshapes the architecture of the DMN, so that the brain's default state becomes more present-centered and attentive.[22]

From this description, it is hopefully apparent that distraction during meditation practice is a necessary ingredient in training the brain to switch out of its DMN. If distractions never arise, you won't get the practice engaging the salience network and switching out of the DMN. And that practice is how meditation reduces self-criticism: less DMN activity means less "selfing" and less judgment. But practice is essential. You must do the reps—practicing over and over—to change those brain habits and to build different connections and processes.

Meditation Leads to Less Judging toward Others

I remember an experience in college, sitting in a circle on the floor of someone's dorm room, talking loosely about our lives and various ideas from our classes. Another student brought up the social psychology phenomenon that "you are your most distinguishing characteristic"—that is, that others view you by whatever aspect seems most striking or unusual. "Right, like twitchy butt girl!" someone said. "Oh yeah, I know twitchy butt girl. She works in the cafeteria, right?" I became paranoid. What was most striking about me? How did people remember me? Was it flattering? Or not so much?

It's our brain's default to judge people rapidly, often even before we're aware that we're doing it. We notice one thing about a person (most likely about their appearance) and then, especially if there are lots of people around or if we also have other things on our minds, we move on. Done. But that over-simplification leads to all kinds of biases—racism, sexism, and ageism among them. Research indicates that meditation leads to lower levels of racism and ageism, because people make fewer automatic associations.[23]

I also suspect that making rapid, automatic judgments about people based on their appearance contributes to loneliness and even self-judgment. When you view other people as one-dimensional supporting actors or extras, it can seem as though you're the only one trying hard to handle a complex and challenging inner life. That false assumption can seem real, and it is quite an isolating one.

The neuroscientist Rick Hanson teaches a mindfulness practice called "See beings, not bodies" that can help break the habit of categorizing, judging, and "thingifying" people.[24] He advises that when you encounter someone, you can try to remember the many different roles that they have (teacher, parent, friend, son, smart, funny, reader of detective novels). You can try to imagine the complexity within their own mind and all of the thoughts and emotions that must be swirling around with them. You might also notice moment-to-moment changes that you observe within yourself (like feeling energized or sleepy, or how pieces of a conversation feel for you). Then, you might consider how moment-to-moment changes are happening for the other person. You can try out this practice with someone who feels "neutral" to you, like a bus driver or café employee, and then with people who are closer to you.

I tried "see beings, not bodies" on a silent weeklong meditation retreat by first noticing my one-dimensional impression of other participants: "purple-haired girl," "tattoo guy," or "wheelchair guy" (I suspected, in my own space of projected judgment, that I was "pregnant woman," fully defined by that feature alone). Then, I consciously tried to notice less obvious things about them: "tattoo guy" reached for the same hot sauce that I preferred; "purple-haired girl" seemed quite skilled at chopping carrots. I also imagined some of the many ways that those other people had lives that were just as multifaceted as mine. I noticed that I felt less lonely when I stepped beyond that urge to judge or label people with only the feature that initially stood out to me.

Meditation can enhance practices such as "see beings, not bodies," since meditation builds the capacity to notice without judging, or at least with less judging. As you notice your breath, you can observe different aspects about it. Maybe some breaths are shorter, longer, a bit shallow, or a bit deeper. Inhaling and exhaling each involve different physical sensations. Judgments and words might arise, but as you meditate, you can practice observing physical sensations by noticing them with your body ("How does this breath feel right now in my body?") rather than with your brain and its labels. Over time, this practice leads to more noticing without labeling and judging.

Handling Self-Criticism during Meditation Practice

Beyond feeling self-critical for losing focus during meditation, there are other ways that self-criticism might emerge. You might dislike the thoughts and feelings that arise—and it might even feel as though you dislike yourself for having them. Or perhaps the issue is more physical. If you find yourself experiencing physical tightness or tension, fidgeting, or falling asleep, you might automatically berate yourself for not meditating correctly. You may be upset about a lack of consistency with your meditation practice, see the normal ups and downs in meditation as a sign that you're doing it wrong, or feel disappointed with yourself that you're not seeing benefits from meditation as quickly as you had hoped. Those are all real, valid feelings; however, they all contain an element of self-criticism in interpreting challenges with meditation as a sign that there's a problem with you or with your practice. During the actual experience of meditating, you have the opportunity to try to notice your own self-criticism—and other challenges—as you practice. Here are a few ways to address self-criticism or other challenges if they arise during meditation:

- *With curiosity.* As you notice your experiences during sitting meditation and how they influence self-talk, you can bring in some curiosity for what's happening when you criticize yourself about meditating. Does beating yourself up for losing focus during meditation reflect an overall sense that you're generally not good enough, not doing enough? Does going there feel familiar, or easy? What are the physical sensations that arise during moments of self-judgment? Can you try noticing them with your body, instead of generating so many thoughts about them?

- *By meditating for longer periods at a time.* Because meditation is so difficult (but often valuable for learning new ways to handle thoughts and experiences), many beginners like to start with about five to ten minutes at a time. But many people (even experienced meditators) find that the mind takes about twenty minutes to settle down, like a snow globe that's been shaken up. Some people even just write off the first twenty minutes as sort of a warm-up. When you're ready, you might block off a time to experiment with sitting for longer than twenty minutes, in case you find that your mind starts to settle down after that time.

- *By changing your goal during meditation.* You might find that you're especially hung up on the idea of staying focused on your breath. What happens if you change your goal from staying focused to instead observing how gently and kindly you're able to accept it when your focus wanders? How calmly can you return your focus? How gently can you return your focus? How nonjudgmentally?

- *By shifting your attention down from your head and into your body.* Okay, so you're paying attention to your breath, but the *way* that you're paying attention might still involve a lot of thinking. And when you're doing a lot of thinking, even about breathing, it's much easier to veer off into other thoughts, like that email you need to write or whether you're meditating right. Can you shift the vantage point of noticing breathing down from your head, so that it's deeper down in your body? Maybe you can get deeper, and more physical, in your noticing.

- *By finding something new in this very moment.* Can you open to noticing something new in this exact moment? Maybe you feel this very breath in the middle of your nose, or its flavor is a bit distinct, or you can observe the breath flowing through different parts of your body. Anything physical in this very moment (the feeling of squinting a bit? Or flexing your toes?), unless you go off and interpret it as meaning something about your life or about the future, can help anchor you into some nowness. And finding new things can also bring hope that we haven't yet seen it all—that we can move away from past habits.

- *By acknowledging with compassion.* Yes, meditation is hard. Changing mental habits is hard. I wouldn't be recommending it without solid evidence that it is indeed possible. But it's hard. I'm sorry about that. Perhaps you can also acknowledge that it is truly difficult, validate that it can be quite frustrating at times, and keep encouraging yourself that it's a process.

- *By noticing what's neutral.* You can tune in to breathing sensations that don't seem particularly "good" or "bad," listen to the sounds around you, or notice aspects of your environment as you walk. During the first week of November 2020, I found myself tied up in knots as I waited for the results of the United States presidential election. I tried to tune in to the fall leaves around me during walking meditation. Yellow. Red. Brown. Green. Pink. Purple. Orange. Gradations in color, contrasting colors. Fluttering, buoyant, steady. It comforted me that the leaves didn't care who won the election; paying attention in a neutral way provided me with a place of refuge, steadying me during that time of turmoil, so that I was less focused on my fears or how I was coping.

- *With patience.* Try to remember that this practice is about building helpful habits over time, like brushing your teeth. The mindfulness teacher Ajahn Brahm advises us not to expect every meditation session to be a "payday." Some sessions might seem uneventful or difficult, and that's okay. During a medical emergency, the teacher Sharon Salzberg noted that her "ordinary practice, like every day, even if it's boring, even if it feels like nothing's happening—that's what carried me in those moments of crisis."[25]

Another way to work with self-criticism and other automatic judgments is to actually try to focus some of your sessions on "not judging judgment." Once you start noticing your automatic judgments on purpose, you might be surprised by how pervasive they are. One friend spent a whole day on a mindfulness retreat where he focused on observing his own judging. Since it's easy to judge your judgments ("I shouldn't be so judgmental; I shouldn't be so hard on myself"), he focused on noticing the judgments in a neutral way, by just observing them. When he described the experience, he was struck by the amount of judging he noticed. "I had a judgment for everything, all day long," he said. "I noticed, 'I'm judging her; I'm judging him; I'm judging the food; I'm judging myself judging.'" As he related the experience to me, I noticed that he didn't seem in pain about how much he was judging. Setting his intention to "just notice" the judging for the time being, rather than trying to stop judging, was liberating.

Fluctuations during Meditation Practice

Sometimes I wish that meditation worked instantly to reduce self-criticism, particularly when I'm recommending it to other people. But it doesn't. Meditation reduces self-judgment very effectively, but it takes time. Most people will need at least a few weeks of regular meditation, and a few months will most likely help much more.

The first few meditation sessions can be rocky. It can be boring and difficult to just sit there and to try to keep your attention on your breath. One student wrote, "It is crazy how sitting still and quiet for fifteen minutes feels so hard and long when I can easily spend an hour scrolling on my phone in what feels like five minutes." The first time I tried it, during a meditation workshop in college, it felt almost unbearable. I wasn't eager to try it again, and so I didn't for a long time. It seemed like tough mental work, and even worse, I felt I wasn't good at it. I thought that I wasn't right for meditation, or it wasn't right for me. But somehow, circling back to meditation in yoga classes years later, I wound up trying again, and again, and again, and it got easier. I felt very physically restless during the first few months of consistent practice; then I worked on noticing the restlessness without judging it or getting up; and finally, my restlessness disappeared.

Even after years of meditating, I have many mental distractions, especially during the "settling down" period at the beginning of a session. I'll be sitting there, trying to focus on the breath, and other thoughts will intrude: an email I have to write, a random memory, or a plan for dinner. I might notice self-judgment ("Why didn't I turn my phone notifications off?"). I frequently experience a "half-and-half" focus, where part of my mind is focused on my breathing and another part is rambling away. In that instance, once I notice, I try to gather the wandering parts of my mind back to focusing on my breath.

Then, in the very next breath, I might observe the pleasant sensation of the way that currents of air move through the room, or have the thought arise that "I have everything I need in this moment." It's a bit of a jumble. Because I'm used to it, the jumble doesn't bother me very much. I know that's just how my mind works. I also experience periods during meditation that seem like less of a jumble, where my practice feels peaceful, steady, insightful, or even transcendent. I know that even if a particular meditation session feels like a bust, what's important is the regular practice of noticing sensations and thoughts, accepting them, and returning my focus.

If you practice meditation several times, you are likely to notice differences in your practice sessions. One of my students commented that "fluctuation is ironically the most consistent part of my mindfulness practices." It's common for beginning meditators to label their meditation practices as "good" and "bad" sessions, especially with respect to the amount of distracting thoughts that they experienced. Over time, and with the experience of viewing many "ups" and "downs" with meditation, judgment about meditation itself seems to soften. One student wrote that "meditation has actually changed the way that I perceive 'bad,' because when I sat with bad feelings from a nonjudgmental state of mind, I truly began to see my failures as learning experiences." Another student described how "easy" and "difficult" moments within meditation seem to emerge with every session:

> If I had to categorize my practices, I do notice that some sessions are bad and some are good, but I would prefer to call it difficult instead of bad, almost a challenge, and the good ones are just easier but not necessarily better. The more difficult ones usually involve restlessness, thinking about how long I have left, or not being able to breathe through my pains and getting sidetracked often. The easier ones usually consist of a feeling of grace, being able to flow through the meditation, and a feeling of groundedness. That being said,

most sessions have both good and bad moments within them, no session has completely been without challenges, and no difficult session has been without benefits. And most importantly, every session has made me better in my everyday life.

You can also choose to change your meditation practice by incorporating different types of meditation or by meditating in different settings. You might try walking meditation, where you pay careful attention to the physical sensations of walking or to the visual scenery around you and return your focus when you become distracted. Many people enjoy guided meditations, in which a teacher provides instructions for breathing meditation, body scan meditations, or otherwise. Meditating in the context of a class, workshop, religious service, or retreat can offer a different kind of engagement with the practice. However you choose to meditate, or even if you choose not to, I hope that you find ways to relate to yourself with more patience, curiosity, and kindness, and with less judgment.

REFLECTION QUESTIONS

1. What sorts of challenges do you anticipate arising as you consider practicing meditation (e.g., boredom, skepticism, frustration)? If you've tried meditation already, what hindrances arose during your practice? How have you handled them?

2. Have you observed any shifts in your judgment over your lifetime? Was there a time when you felt yourself being less judgmental, more judgmental, or judgmental about different things than you are now?

3. Are there thoughts and feelings that you have that feel unacceptable? For instance, do you prevent yourself from feeling certain emotions such as anger or sadness?

4. How much mental energy do you use judging yourself? How often does it feature as part of your day or momentary experience? Do you anticipate any benefits from reducing your self-judgment?

5. Can you notice moments when your default mode network is activated, moments when your task positive network is activated, or moments when you are switching out of the default mode network on purpose?

6. Do you notice any self-criticism arise during meditation practice? If so, can you notice it gently, and then redirect your mental focus?

4

Fail Forward, or Act
Before You Think

I love this one: "Fail early, fail often, fail forward." You
know, it's always a little bit frustrating to me when people have a negative relationship with failure. Failure is a
massive part of being able to be successful. . . . You gotta
take a shot, you have to live at the edge of your capabilities.
You've got to live where you're almost certain you're going
to fail. That's the reason for practice. Practice is controlled
failure; you're getting to your limit until you get to the
point where all of a sudden, your body makes the adjustment and then you can do it. Failure actually helps you to
recognize the areas where you need to evolve. So fail early,
fail often, fail forward.

—*Will Smith (2018)*

WHICH COMES FIRST, action or thought? Those of us who
struggle with self-criticism might assume that thoughts always come first. Self-critical thinking, including the fear of
failure, can paralyze us, keeping us from acting in alignment
with our deepest values. It's hard to start an exercise program,

apply for a new job, or invite someone to lunch when your mind automatically worries that you'll mess it up. Instead of waiting to feel better about yourself before you take action, this chapter asks you to flip it around: to act first and think later. Healthy actions can lead to healthy self-talk, especially if the actions are specific, scheduled, and consistent.

Motivation, confidence, and well-being can all arise from repeated positive actions. For instance, regular acts of service form a central part of many religious and spiritual traditions. The idea is that service itself—the action rather than the intention—cultivates positive internal states. Instead of waiting to become generous before helping others, people become generous through helping others. This route, from behavior to belief, can also work for people who believe that they just can't begin dating, write a short story, or make a homemade pie.

Psychology professors sometimes draw a triangle on the chalkboard and label its vertices "thoughts," "feelings," and "behavior." Each domain affects the others. For instance, self-critical thoughts ("I'm not very good at making friends") could lead to feeling sad and to refraining from socializing. Or it could go the other way; that is, refraining from socializing could lead to feeling more anxious about it.

The interrelationships between thoughts, feelings, and behavior also operate when you're trying to improve well-being. However, it's hard to just have (and truly believe) a healthier thought or to generate a more pleasant feeling. Going right to the behavior can be a very effective strategy if you can tolerate that you might not actually feel motivated. You might ask yourself, "What would I be doing each day if I felt better about myself?" Can you go straight to doing some of those actions, without waiting for the self-criticism to disappear first? You may find that self-criticism abates after the new behaviors are in place.

"Act before you think" is a strategy for managing the kind of self-criticism that interferes with your goals. The saying "Think before you act" (sometimes extended to add "and twice before you speak") relates to actions that could hurt you or someone else. So, when I encourage people to "act before you think," I'm not suggesting that you explode at people or spend money that you don't have. Rather, prioritizing positive actions can help you get ahead of the self-criticism that impedes them—the self-doubt that stops you before you even get started.

Prioritizing action can help allay a fear of failure. Fear of failure is a common facet of self-criticism. Sometimes feelings of failure are propelled by something else that does need our attention, such as a loss that needs to be grieved. But most of the time, failure is a normal part of learning a new skill. And in that case, staying fixated on failure is a big impediment. We need to be able to tolerate it or learn from it, and not just quit or never get started. Athletes, musicians, and chefs all understand that failure is part of the process of learning a new technique, piece of music, or dish. Being a caring parent or partner also involves a willingness to make and repair mistakes. Confidence arises from learning from the problem and trying again rather than withdrawing or believing those self-critical voices that rush to interpret failure as meaning there's something wrong with you. Deepening attention and curiosity toward your actions in the moment can help you persist, and it may also cause the fear of failure and other aspects of self-criticism to recede.

The idea is to act despite the presence of self-criticism. You will need to think a bit, however, about which actions you want to take and how you plan to make them specific, regular, and consistent. As you approach action in a new way to transform self-criticism, it can be helpful to allow yourself room for uncertainty and even failure, to hold a growth mindset as you act, and to be brave rather than ashamed in sharing setbacks and in accepting support.

———

The artist Stephanie Krimmel describes an innovative method she uses to build the habit of creating every day. After two decades of work in the technology industry, she knew she wanted a change. But changing her professional identity required some new approaches, and she felt unsure about how to get started. She explained,

> I really wasn't giving myself permission to be lost or explore. I guess I felt "not knowing" was a sign of weakness, or at least it was really uncomfortable for me. At some point I figured that I'd be less uncomfortable by doing something, and that by doing something I'd be learning something, or at least *trying* something. One of the things I decided to try was digital painting on the iPad. I bought myself an iPad and an Apple pencil, loaded some painting apps, and then did nothing with it for nearly a month. My excuse for this was that I didn't have a case for the iPad and didn't want anything to happen to it, but I think the underlying reason I didn't start is that I wasn't sure how.

I decided that I would start by "playing around" with digital painting for six minutes a day. On the first day, I started by sketching the lilies on my patio, and was surprised when the six-minute timer rang—the time seemed to go by so fast! That first painting wasn't a masterpiece by any means, but I noticed that I really enjoyed creating it. So on the following day, I made another, and another on the next day. I've continued the daily practice of making digital paintings ever since then; it's now something I've done nearly every day for almost two years.

The artwork has changed quite a bit over those years, and so have my attitudes. I've given myself permission to not know. These days, the unknown is something I relish, rather than fear, because it means I get to explore and learn new things. I find myself seeking out discomfort rather than avoiding it. I feel a lot more courageous and much freer than I used to.[1]

Stephanie doesn't wait until she feels an idea or project she's sure is worthwhile emerges. Instead, her behavior leads her to feel more confident. Her process also reflects the importance of having a specific routine—in her case, six minutes a day—rather than a vague intention to create art. Stephanie's emphasis on exploration, rather than self-evaluation, allows her to try new things. Her reflection also indicates a deep engagement with the action of creating art, which might have been reinforced by the time limit. Finally, she shows persistence in keeping up the habit for several years and by recognizing the benefits of the behavior.

Core Exercise

Pick an activity that you think you might enjoy but that contains some novel element that makes it different from something you've done before. Schedule the new activity for at least once a week. Then actually do the activity; make mistakes; praise your *effort* rather than the result; and keep trying, over and over.

Leapfrogging, or Doing Active Things When You Don't Feel Like It

One of the best techniques for reducing depression (which is, of course, a mental state that usually includes a ton of self-criticism along with prominent feelings of failure) has a fancy name: *behavioral activation*. I often explain behavioral activation as "doing active stuff even when you don't feel like it." The "active stuff" can be anything that isn't sedentary or passive: gardening, hiking, dancing, trying a new recipe, or socializing. Studies have shown that behavioral activation is a highly effective strategy for improving mental health.[2] Instead of waiting for motivation to do something, you do it first. Motivation often follows. In fact, research indicates that behavioral changes, like quitting smoking, often begin with taking action rather than going through a long period of contemplation and planning.[3]

Behavioral activation works well for a few different reasons. By prioritizing action above thoughts and feelings, change can happen more quickly. Once you separate out "doing the thing" from "feeling like doing the thing" or "won-

of just one minute of exercise, like being in the gym, dedicated stretching time, or running. What would be necessary to make that one minute happen? Can we problem-solve any potential obstacles? I remember one student who wanted to resume running, but his running shoes were at his parents' house instead of in his dorm room. Addressing this specific barrier helped him start running again and to feel better about himself. Action was needed, rather than an in-depth analysis of his lack of motivation and other internal obstacles.

Sometimes I call this intervention "foot out the door." It's a reminder to focus less on how you feel emotionally—particularly with respect to motivation—and to emphasize instead the action of your foot getting outside your home. If physical exercise doesn't seem like the right fit for you, I encourage you to start or continue other activities that reflect your interests and values. You might choose to take a class, learn a new language, or volunteer your skills at a food bank, tutoring center, or animal shelter. Whether your behavioral activation is exercise-based or not, it can help to choose an activity that requires you to be somewhere at a specific time in the company of other people. That way, it's less likely that you will put it off, and you'll get the added benefit of combining some social interaction with the behavior.

Increasing positive behaviors can go a long way toward improving depression, anxiety, and other challenges related to self-criticism. However, things don't always go smoothly. You might become injured, the Japanese class you loved might end, or the reupholstering project you started might turn out to be much harder than you anticipated. In those cases, you might remind yourself that setbacks are a normal part of life. One way to get comfortable with failure is to pick activities that actually require it.

Failure Is a Feature, Not a Bug

Working with college students, both in the therapy room and in the classroom, has left me with deep impressions about how our culture trains young people to view failure. By the time they get to college, most students have insulated themselves from failure to the point where they're predominantly engaged in classes and activities that they feel that they are "good" at. If you ask a four-year-old to draw you a picture, sing you a song, or dance, they'll probably do so, as long as they're in the right mood. We all start out accepting mistakes as part of the learning process. You can't learn to walk or talk before doing both incorrectly, thousands of times. I like to imagine the baby who says, "Well, that didn't work out. Other people are walkers, but it seems like I'm just not one of them. I guess I'll just lie here on the floor."

But after we're done being a baby, or perhaps a toddler, we seem to lose our tolerance for mistakes, to the point that it's a huge challenge to accept failure as a normal part of life. School exposes us to an onslaught of judgment that sorts kids into those who are "good at" sports, "good at" music, and "good at" art. By college, then, most kids have learned to self-select into only activities that they feel "good" at. Failure is so painful. Many of my students seem to question the value of trying something new or taking a risk getting to know someone they may not like. It seems easier to continue the activities that they're comfortable with and that have minimal risk of failure. To feel successful, it's common to compartmentalize instances of failure, to keep failure away from their own sense of identity. We make failure foreign.

These students—and the rest of us—can benefit from

learning to accept and handle failure. But it's hard to unlearn our strategies for avoiding failure and instead become willing to fail. The journey involves action; it requires the lived experience of failing and tolerating failure.

If one of the flavors of your self-talk is a very low threshold for tolerating failure, I highly recommend sitting meditation (to be honest, I highly recommend sitting meditation for a lot of stuff). Meditation, by which I mean any formal practice implementing a specific mindfulness technique such as paying attention to your breathing, involves practicing over and over again. Part of that practice is the art of refocusing. You try to focus, you lose focus, and you try to refocus without judging yourself for losing focus. Repeat. Repeat. Repeat. Repeat. Repeat again a thousand times.

You can't actually get "better" at maintaining your focus during meditation—or, maybe I'll say, it can't actually become easier to refocus without beating yourself up—until you've done it a few hundred times, or a few thousand. Those "failures" are necessary in order to learn how to return your focus without judging, and to make returning your focus easier. But over time, something shifts. Becoming distracted stops being such a big deal. You get used to losing your focus and returning it. As you become less self-critical about it, you become less self-critical in general.

I try to normalize the process of "failing" during meditation—that is, losing focus, becoming restless, and observing the impulse to criticize yourself. That was what I had to do. I was an undergraduate the first time I tried meditation, and I found it excruciating—extremely difficult and boring. My comfort with meditation grew only slowly during my first few months of daily sitting.

Having practiced a good deal with failing at focusing during meditation, I'm more and more willing to acknowledge and repair mistakes with my partner and kids. I talk openly about being wrong, making mistakes, and being willing to fail. It's to the point that my three-year-old son has started to ask me each morning, in a way that seems more curious than judgmental, "Mama, what are you going to be wrong about today?"

If meditation is not your thing, try something else that you're bound to fail with, like cooking new recipes or playing a new sport or instrument. Practice failing with more curiosity than judgment toward the failure. Action is crucial here. It's not just about choosing a new attitude but purposefully re-creating the lived experience of failure and accepting failure, over and over again. This isn't just mindset; it's mindset plus practice.

It's easier to practice failing forward with things like focusing on your breathing or trying a new hobby than with things that are more highly charged, such as paid work or personal relationships. Becoming comfortable with failure for those lesser-charged activities generalizes to the more highly charged domains.

The mindfulness teacher Tara Brach suggests deepening attention to the present moment to handle fear of failure, because fearing failure involves projecting ourselves into a hypothetical future. This is part of the reason that many coaches encourage their players' mindfulness practices. They want players to keep their minds in the game instead of being distracted by their worries about what will happen and what that would mean. Athletes who undergo training in mindfulness techniques report more moments of "flow" or "being in the zone," as well as improved performance.[5]

Overinterpreting Events as Failures

In 1964, the astronomers Arno Penzias and Robert Wilson wanted to investigate long-distance radiation in the Milky Way. They revamped an old radio telescope to make it exceedingly sensitive. However, they heard a constant background noise that prevented them from making the kinds of observations that they had hoped. Unclear what the sound was or how to make it stop, they became terribly frustrated. Perhaps it was interference from nearby New York City, or weather-related static. And then there were the pigeons: a pair of them had nested in the receiver, and they were spreading droppings and other pigeon-related debris.

Penzias and Wilson tried to fix the buzz or to work around it for *over a year.* They got rid of the pigeons and scrubbed out the pigeon poop. (I confirmed that they actually scrubbed out the poop themselves—as new hires, they didn't have postdoctoral or graduate students helping them.) They hoped for changes in the weather. But they still couldn't find the subtle signals they were trying to detect. The static was constant, without fluctuations, and emanating from all parts of the sky. It didn't make sense as an artifact of the weather, city sounds, or birds. Then Penzias happened to run into another astronomer, Bernard Burke, on an airplane. Burke suggested that Penzias consult Bob Dicke, a theoretical physicist at Princeton University.

As soon as Penzias described the sound, Dicke knew what it was. He and others had hypothesized that a radio telescope with enough sensitivity could pick up radiation left over from the big bang approximately fourteen billion years ago. He and his colleagues had already begun to look for this radiation, or cosmic microwave background (CMB), and they planned to build their own dish to find it. ("Boys, we've been scooped," Dicke apparently said to his team.) Penzias and Wilson received the 1978 Nobel Prize in Physics for their work, which provided the first direct evidence of the big bang and set the stage for learning much more about how and when the universe began, its components, and the speed of its expansion.

There's a lot to love about this story. Somehow the pigeon poop seems especially poignant. That is, the astronomers not only had no idea that the sound that they heard was a huge, Nobel Prize–worthy discovery. They literally thought it was poop. Their story for that first year is a classic instance of misinterpreting an event as a failure. The phenomenon itself (the buzz) didn't change. The only thing that changed was the mental interpretation: this static isn't poop, it's the sound of the big bang!

I've asked students in my psychology classes to consider experiences that felt like a failure at the time but that ultimately benefited them. Their discussions brim with examples of "failed" relationships that clarified their own priorities, failed assignments that led them to new study habits or sources of support, and sports injuries that led them to develop other strengths and interests. Their examples were from the past, but I think it's possible to consider the present moment, and to ask: What seems like a failure or setback right now but could be a source of growth in disguise?

Transforming a Fixed Mindset into a Growth Mindset

By now it's been well established: having a "growth mindset" rather than a "fixed mindset" in terms of your own abilities is strongly connected with happiness and success. Instead of thinking "I'm good at this" or "I'm terrible at that," having perspectives such as "I can learn from this experience" or "I can get better at this with practice" are far more adaptive and connected with higher levels of well-being. A "growth mindset" can be a powerful component of healthy self-talk.

Much of the research on this topic has come from Carol Dweck, a psychologist at Stanford University. Dweck encourages people to notice their own mixture of "fixed" and "growth" mindsets; to understand how their mindsets developed; to observe self-talk related to their mindsets; and to take growth-oriented action to change self-talk about both goals and assumed limitations. We often absorb cultural messages about how gender or race might affect our achievements, even on an unconscious level, but growth-mindset training can improve self-sabotaging related to those problematic beliefs.[6]

Ibram Kendi, author of *How to Be an Antiracist*, describes how the culture around him contributed to a fixed mindset:

> I thought I was a subpar student and was bombarded by messages—from Black people, White people, the media—that told me that the reason was rooted in my race . . . which made me more discouraged and less motivated as a student . . . which only further reinforced for me the racist idea that Black people just weren't very studious . . . which made me feel even more despair or indifference.[7]

A fixed mindset might influence your thinking and behaviors in a hidden way, or it might show up as sabotaging self-criticism. Dweck asked people to tell her about what it sounds like when their "fixed-mindset personas" arrive inside of their minds. One person observed that, "when I'm under pressure, my fixed-mindset persona appears. He fills my head with noise and keeps me from paying attention to the work I have to do . . . he makes comments like, 'You don't have the ability to grasp difficult concepts. You have reached your limit.'" Another respondent explained that their fixed-mindset persona "doesn't allow me to take risks that may affect our reputation as a successful person. She doesn't let me speak out for fear of being wrong. She forces me to look like a person who can understand and do everything effortlessly."[8]

So, how do you actually change your mindset? With a little self-talk change plus a lot of behavior change.

As you consider making a shift in your mindset, you might pause to acknowledge, in a compassionate way, just how hard it is to change mindsets. There can be a real sense of loss in giving up fixed ideas about your identity and self-esteem. Dweck writes, "It's especially not easy to replace it with a mindset that tells you to embrace all the things that have felt threatening: challenge, struggle, criticism, setbacks."[9]

Deciding that you want a "growth mindset" is great, but that decision alone doesn't seem sufficient to make it happen—you need to push yourself to take concrete, behavioral action and to reinforce those actions. Most of the people who have a "growth mindset" had others around them who praised their efforts and who encouraged persistence and creativity—over and over and over, so that "growth mindset" brain circuits became established. For those of us who weren't so lucky, we can learn how to provide that kind of positive encouragement to ourselves.

Quintin Cutts, a professor of computer science education at the University of Glasgow, and his colleagues noted that students often dropped out of introductory programming classes.[10] So Cutts and his team implemented a three-part intervention: (1) tutors described the growth mindset to students; (2) students received growth-mindset feedback on their work; and (3) when they got stuck, students were encouraged to use a worksheet that pointed them to different pathways to solve problems. The team found that students' mindsets and test scores improved with this multifaceted intervention, a result that reflects the power of combining actions (the students kept trying new strategies, even when they were stuck) with encouraging growth-mindset messages.

In practicing a growth mindset, it seems to help to choose manageable, concrete tasks that involve some element of failing and trying again. Students who are taught action-based tools to tackle the task at hand (including breaking up pieces of work into smaller chunks, building good work habits, and regulating emotions) have better outcomes.[11] In an interesting set of research studies, Stefano Palminteri and his colleagues observed that the opportunity to learn from mistakes promotes activity in a region of the brain (the ventral striatum) that differs from the part of the brain that is activated when we attempt to avoid mistakes (anterior insula).[12] This means that handling failure, rather than avoiding it, might change some of the brain's default habits.

To become more comfortable with failure, it can help to pick something new and specific, so that you have an actual lived experience rather than a vague intention. It's fine to pick exercise, but if you've exercised before, pick a new type of exercise (e.g., yoga, rock climbing, rowing, qi gong) that you haven't tried before. If you like cooking and want to investigate that further, pick a kind of cooking that's new to you (Thai cuisine; soufflés; recipes that use a slow cooker or an instant pot), one that involves making dishes you have never made before. The same goes for a musical instrument or type of art.

Just pick something; do it at least twice a week; and praise your effort (not the results) for at least a few minutes a day, every day (even on days where you aren't engaging in the activity). Keep trying and persisting and praising your effort and then putting in more effort, over and over, even amid mistakes or failures, for several weeks, to develop and reinforce a growth mindset. If you like, you can pepper in supportive phrases like, "This is hard; I'm just going to try it," "It's more important that I try it than if I succeed," or "It's brave and good for me to try new things, even if it feels uncomfortable." Or—of course—"Inhale, my friend; exhale, my friend," as described in chapter 1. It's important to note that you are going for "process praise" (praising your process and your effort) rather than "person praise" (praising your skill, accomplishments, or attributes).[15]

Usually, it takes time. Dweck does recount several stories of people who were taught the growth mindset and report that it made a huge difference in their lives right away. (And if that's the case for you, fantastic!) But several studies that demonstrate mindset shifts involve more substantial training in the growth mindset over longer periods of time—often trainings last six or more weeks or involve ongoing meetings or support relationships.[14]

Growth-mindset interventions that teach how the brain works—that is, that we build new physical pathways in our brain by trying and learning new things—seem to be particularly helpful. Research demonstrates that it's fabulous for the adult brain to learn a new sport or a new musical instrument: the combination of practicing new ways of thinking, new ways of moving your hands or body, and new hand-eye coordination are all extremely good for our brains.

Growth mindsets initiate a self-reinforcing spiral. That is, you might start by taking action to try new things and to persist when they get hard. This in turn makes you feel more confident and competent about trying new things and persisting, which then contributes to having a "growth mindset" in which you view yourself as able to learn, grow, and persist. This then contributes to your success and happiness, which reinforces subsequent efforts, engagement, and willingness to try new things . . . and the cycle continues.

I hope it's clear by now that the central element of cultivating a growth mindset is growth-oriented *action*. To change mindsets, decide what growth-oriented action you want to take in your life, and then do it. In a section of her book *Mindset: The New Psychology of Success* called "feeling bad, but doing good," Dweck notes that "vowing is useless" and advises readers to "make a concrete, growth-oriented plan, and stick to it."[15]

Overidentification with Failure

It's much easier to accept failure if we interpret it as a normal part of being human, as a necessary part of learning and growth, or as a neutral event. It's much harder to accept failure if we interpret it as meaning something terrible about ourselves. Believing "I feel anxious because I'm an anxious person" doesn't leave much room for change. Conversely, believing that "anxiety is a something that I often experience" leaves all kinds of room for exploration and experimentation.

The executive Leigh Morgan described a painful time in which she realized that she didn't fit into the culture of the large pharmaceutical company that employed her. She recalled, "It was a hard time for me, in this role, feeling a bit like a misfit, 'what's wrong with me?' Had I not had that struggle, and felt that dissonance, I wouldn't have the knowledge of, 'Oh, I need to look for roles in organizations where there's a cultural fit, and where the values of the organization are consistent enough with my values, so that every day I can show up and say, we're rolling in the same direction in a manner that really lights my fire.' It helped me fine-tune my mental radar, my heart radar, and my spirit radar."[16]

The mindfulness teacher Pema Chödrön offers her own story:

> The worst time in my life was when I felt like the greatest failure, and this had to do with a second failed marriage. I had never experienced such vulnerability and pain than during that particular groundless, rug-pulled-out experience. And I really felt bad about myself.
>
> Sometimes you experience failed expectations as heartbreak and disappointment, and sometimes you feel rage. But at that time, instead of doing the habitual thing of labeling yourself a "failure" or a "loser" or thinking there is something wrong with you, you could get curious about what is going on. Getting curious about outer circumstances and how they are impacting you, noticing what words come out and what your internal discussion is—this is the key.[17]

The writer Bronwen Tate describes another self-talk method for dissolving overidentification: humility. She writes,

What became clear to me was the need for humility to let me be kind to myself. I think the key phrase that shifted my self-talk was "who am I to never _____?" So, if I forget something or have a cringing moment or disappoint myself, I pause and say "Okay, I'm human. Who am I to never forget anything?" or "Who am I to never make a mistake?" That reminder of humility allows me to let go and not obsess about the mistake.[18]

Sharing Failure and Perseverance as a Form of Generosity

I've missed over 9,000 shots in my career. I've lost almost 300 games. Twenty-six times I've been trusted to take the game-winning shot and missed. I've failed over and over and over again in my life. And that is why I succeed.

—*Michael Jordan*

Michael Jordan didn't have to share his failure stats in the quote above. He could have glossed over them. But instead, he offered up details along with these powerful words—words that portray a deep acceptance of failure, an understanding that failure is necessary, and a willingness to keep on going within a context that always includes failure. It's an act of kindness for him to share the wisdom of his acceptance of failure. His attitude toward failure can be a source of hope and inspiration for anyone who hears it. He shows that it's possible to share failure in a constructive way rather than in a self-deprecating manner.

The Princeton psychology professor Johannes Haushofer explained that he created and shared a personal "CV of failures" with the intention of enlightening other people about the ubiquity and necessity of failure.[19] This approach isn't just about helping others—it can also lead to more intimacy and trust. Indeed, the Harvard Business School professor Dr. Alison Wood Brooks and her colleagues found that talking about current and past failures can lead to closer relationships with colleagues.[20] The idea that talking about failure can promote community is reflected in the initiative of author and entrepreneur Leticia Gasca, the cofounder of #FuckupNights, a multinational program for entrepreneurs to share their experiences of failure and to learn from others' failure experiences.

Siddhartha Gautama, the prince who eventually became the Buddha (the enlightened one), tried many methods of seeking enlightenment that didn't work. He refrained from eating or sleeping, and he tried relating to his own mind in a forceful manner by attempting to "beat down, constrain, and crush mind with mind." As he tried out each method of seeking "sublime peace," he remained open to fail; that is, to answer "no" to the question, "Could that be the path to awakening?"[21] Even if he did have moments of doubt or challenging self-talk, his actions show that he kept going anyway. Eventually, Siddhartha remembered a mental state that he'd experienced as a child, when he sat under a rose apple tree. It was a pleasant and balanced state of presence, with a peaceful quality of mind. The memory of that state set him on a new path and an affirmative answer to the question, "Could this be the path to enlightenment?"

Every year, the University of Washington's Resilience Lab hosts a "Fail Forward" event, where faculty and community leaders share their personal stories of "setbacks, failures, and face plants." It's an extremely popular event—standing room only—that seems to resonate deeply with all who listen.

I recall one year when the university's president, Ana Mari Cauce, was among the speakers. Cauce explained that after her family fled to the United States from Cuba when she was three years old, feelings of being "other" arose from multiple sources, including people who assumed that she was a "poor scholarship kid" or that her childhood home had no books. She described lingering self-doubt, even amid her other accomplishments:

> I did college at home, University of Miami; a good Cuban girl does not leave home. I got into Yale [for graduate school]. My first time in an Anglo setting, I realized I sit too close to people, and I was one of the few people in my class who didn't come from an Ivy. I was lonely. I was scared. I didn't get the job that I wanted when I graduated. I not only didn't get the position, but the University of Washington president told me I wasn't cut out for a leadership position. Those doubts about what it means to be a leader, what a leader looks like, are still there with me today."[22]

I could almost see the impact of Cauce's words as they sank into the sea of students. It looked as though they were thinking, "If the president of the university doubts her abilities, and yet somehow she's made it to where she is, then maybe it's okay that I feel overwhelmed and that I doubt myself sometimes. Maybe those feelings don't actually mean that I can't succeed."

Because most of us hide our failures, it's easy to feel alone in failure and embarrassed about it. We've somehow managed to knit failure up with shame and with loneliness. I'm sure that the kids who attended Cauce's talk felt less alone hearing her discuss her own struggles and failures. And beyond that, she provided them with a gem of a strategy: Keep going. Do the actions that reflect your values rather than waiting for self-doubt or self-criticism to disappear first. Act before you think.

Perhaps "keep going" sounds too simple to be the solution to the complex problems and dramas that we encounter as we try to make our way through life. But deep down I think we all know it: persistence matters as much as, and usually more than, anything else in our quests for success. Very often the issue isn't our ability to keep going, to take the next little step, but the obstacles we place in our way through self-criticism.

Developing healthy self-talk about failing forward might involve figuring out what kind of failure you're facing and investigating how your current self-talk and other perceptions about it might influence you. But unlike other exercises in your self-talk repertoire, the main stretch in failing forward is external action. Truly engage in your new activity, make it happen, and repeat. Do the reps. No matter what flavor of failure you're coping with, there is some way to learn from it, some way to fail forward.

REFLECTION QUESTIONS

1. What is your reaction to the idea of putting some new actions in place—actions that align with your goals and values, and that contain opportunities to fail and to try again?

2. Does your self-talk include a fear of failure or the tendency to interpret failure as meaning there's something wrong with you?

3. What activities are interesting to you, but a sense of "not being good at it" is holding you back from pursuing them?

4. Can you give yourself permission to make a lot of mistakes as you explore a new activity or skill?

5. What does it feel like for you to praise your own effort and persistence rather than results or accomplishments? How does it feel both in the moment and after a week or so of praising effort rather than results?

6. Is there an activity or new habit (like daily flossing, or calling at least one friend per day) that you want to set in motion but somehow it seems too difficult? Can you identify the benefits that you would anticipate from changing your behavior? What concrete steps would you need to take to make the behavior happen (for instance, a reminder alarm)? Can you go do it, repeat it, keep doing it, and reinforce yourself with kind self-talk that acknowledges your effort rather than the accomplishment or result?

5

Training Friendliness with Lovingkindness Meditation

THE JETWAY WAS FREEZING, or technically quite a bit *below* freezing, as I waited to board a plane from Minneapolis, Minnesota, to Madison, Wisconsin, in mid-February. The line wasn't moving, and everyone seemed tense and irritated. My thoughts, and perhaps those of my fellow passengers, were, "I'm freezing! I need to get on this plane right now! I hate this! When will the line start moving?"

Then I remembered that I could practice a specific skill right in that very moment. It's called lovingkindness meditation, and it involves silently repeating kind wishes in order to cultivate feelings of friendliness and goodwill, and to protect the mind against fear and rumination. Since I'd practiced it many times before, I got in the groove pretty easily once I chose to do it. I focused on each person on the Jetway, one at a time—trying not to stare too obviously. I held each person in my thoughts for a few moments as I silently repeated the phrases: "May you be safe. May you be happy. May you be healthy. May you live with ease." I hoped that each person would have a pleasant trip and that the rest of their days, and their lives, would go well.

In under five minutes, my mood was transformed. I didn't feel irritated anymore. I actually felt happy! I was no longer focused on the cold or desperate to get on the plane. My mood was light and calm. The people around me no longer seemed like objects or obstacles, taking up space and slowing things down. These strangers became more complex and more real to me, which somehow led me to relax. Maybe my own feelings of discomfort and impatience didn't feel so overpowering when I imagined each of my fellow passengers' days and lives unfolding as well as possible. It wasn't me against them, in a contest to get comfortable. It felt more balanced and easy, and somehow less terribly cold.

How might such a practice help reduce self-criticism? The practice of lovingkindness meditation (LKM for short) is meant to generate a deep attitude of friendliness toward yourself, others, and all beings. An attitude of friendliness isn't compatible with harsh self-criticism, so there is an element of replacing one habit (self-criticism) with another (kind wishes). Like many other forms of meditation, LKM also trains attention. When you repeat specific words several times, on purpose, it's harder for the mind to wander, ruminate, and elaborate upon the general theme of "I suck." Practicing LKM for yourself helps to replace the habit of self-criticism with one of acceptance and friendliness, and practicing LKM for other people can diminish the sense of separateness that self-criticism creates.

Where self-criticism is alienating, LKM is unifying. It reflects a sense of common humanity, a recognition that all beings have some shared goals. When you use LKM to generate kind wishes toward others, you're also revising how you relate to people in general. Self-criticism often involves comparing your accomplishments or attributes to those of others or fearing that others will judge you poorly. Wishing others well changes that adversarial, competitive, or fearful stance to one that recognizes that we're all in this together, trying to have happy and healthy lives.

And where self-criticism can perpetuate a cascade of difficult fears, memories, and feelings, LKM helps regulate emotions. When I found myself worrying about how my son was adjusting to day care, I repeated LKM phrases for him, and I felt calmer. When walking by a residence for older adults, I saw an elderly woman through the window, dining alone. I silently repeated my wishes that she would feel healthy, happy, and loved. As I generated both of these wishes, instead of fretting about the unknowns—"Is he okay? Is she okay?"—my LKM practice brought a sense of resolution in the moment. Even though I didn't know the full story, I connected with my own good wishes, like having a mental shelter in which to take refuge. In fact, the use of LKM to regulate emotions goes back to some of its earliest origins, including a story in which the Buddha taught LKM as a way for monks to handle their fear of creatures in the forest. And it's often used as a form of protection—increasing love as an antidote to fear.[1]

More than any other practice, LKM often strikes beginners as weird, corny, or stupid. I mean, really. I'm going to repeat some phrases—that I perhaps don't even truly feel at this time—and somehow they'll lead to important changes? Saying something doesn't automatically make it happen. I think of the Seinfeld character Frank Costanza, played brilliantly by the late Jerry Stiller, brimming over with strain and rage as he screams, "SERENITY NOW!"

But my students, and plenty of other people, report that

LKM works, even when they were convinced it wouldn't. Even when they thought it was silly or uncomfortable, they still observed benefits after a few weeks of practice. It's hard for many Westerners to think about kindness as a quality that can be developed. You're either a kind person or not so much, right? If that's your attitude, then it seems strange to repeat phrases that you don't necessarily feel in this moment. However, the available research evidence demonstrates that LKM can improve mental health, self-criticism, and feelings about other people. One of my students offered this description of initial doubts about LKM and subsequent experiences practicing it:

> At first, I was quite skeptical of this practice. I wasn't sure how repeating a phrase would change my feelings toward myself or others. But as I did it, and genuinely offering myself and other people feelings of positivity and kindness, I noticed a very calming sensation fall over me. It was a feeling of contentedness I normally feel after an especially good and fulfilling experience. On the days I practiced LKM in the morning, often before class or work, I noticed that I felt more positive throughout the day.

In the pages ahead, I'll address some common questions about LKM, provide some background about the origins of LKM, describe some of the research showing that it's effective, and share various stories of how this practice has worked for my students and others.

The Meaning of Lovingkindness

The word *lovingkindness* is unusual. It's an attempt to convey a certain kind of love. It's a translation of the word *metta* (or *mettā* in Pali—the original language of Buddhist texts) that expresses this kind of love as well as the practices to cultivate it. The word *metta* is thought to come from a similar word, *mitra*, which refers to friendliness, goodwill, benevolence, affection, kindness, nonviolence, and taking an active interest in other people.

It is completely fine to think of the idea as *friendliness* or *goodwill* if the term *lovingkindness* seems unwieldy or mushy to you, or if you simply prefer other words. "Friendliness" and "goodwill" are just as apt translations of the idea. The meditation teacher Bhante Gunaratana uses the term "loving-friendliness."[2] Even though "lovingkindness" and "lovingkindness meditation" have become common ways for English speakers to refer to the idea and to its practice, some meditation teachers prefer the term "goodwill," perhaps because it conveys a balanced sense of wishing well, without expecting that a positive outcome will occur.

"Goodwill" or "lovingkindness" doesn't mean that you think everything is going well or that you intend to nurture a close personal relationship with everyone. The mindfulness teacher Sharon Salzberg clarifies that "to send loving-kindness does not mean that we approve or condone all actions, it means that we can see clearly actions that are incorrect or unskillful and still not lose the connection."[3] The Buddhist teacher Thanissaro Bhikkhu explains that the term "goodwill" reflects the perspective of wishing well while also recognizing that other people will need to find happiness for themselves and to cultivate skillful actions.[4] He notes that the perspective of goodwill can allow care toward people and nonhuman animals for whom it might not be wise for you to be with in close physical proximity. That might include people whom you have harmed, those who have harmed you, or nonhuman animals who prefer not to be around humans.

Origins of Lovingkindness Meditation

The idea that repeated mental efforts can cultivate a quality of friendliness is an old idea, one that predates Buddhism and Christianity. References to the importance of goodwill, loving-friendliness, or lovingkindness can be found in the Hindu Upanishads (a set of spiritual teachings from India written between 800 and 500 B.C.E.), and in the sutras or spiritual texts of Jainism (ca. 600–300 B.C.E.). It was in this historical and spiritual context that Siddhartha Gautama, born sometime between 624 and 448 B.C.E. and known as the Buddha, developed and described the cultivation of loving-friendliness or lovingkindness.

The Buddha delivered two discourses, or *suttas*, on metta that describe how to cultivate and maintain lovingkindness. The discourses include the excerpts below and explain metta as a capacity that can and should be developed:

This is what should be done
By one who is skilled in goodness,

. . . .
Wishing: In gladness and in safety,
May all beings be at ease.

. . . .
So with a boundless heart
Should one cherish all living beings;
Radiating kindness over the entire world:

. . . .

One should sustain this recollection.
This is said to be the sublime abiding.[5]

It's unclear how the Buddha, or the Hindu teachers before his time, exactly meant metta to be practiced—that is, what the exact phrases or techniques were that the teachers taught in order to cultivate metta. Some Buddhist monastics and others do recite a full version of the "Metta Sutta" (about forty-two lines) one or more times a day. Many Western mindfulness teachers encourage the repetition of four phrases that are shorter and easier, such as: "May I be safe. May I be happy. May I be healthy. May I live with ease." People are often encouraged to repeat the phrases for several minutes at a time while also imagining light or warmth in the area of the heart and visualizing the person to whom they are directing friendly wishes.

The intention behind the words is to consciously try to stay in the zone of lovingkindness: to "sustain this recollection" of wishing all beings well through effort and repetition. Another Buddhist phrase often used in relation to this practice is "sublime abiding," which means that wishing everyone well can become a home in your mind. It's a place to stay, to contemplate, and to marinate, rather than a passing idea.

You don't have to be Buddhist to practice LKM, and you don't have to practice the phrases in a religious way in order to benefit from them. Within its Buddhist context, the quality of metta is meant to be cultivated alongside other internal capacities (including enhancing concentration, developing ethics and virtues, and sharing in others' joy). These capacities are thought to complement each other. However, LKM phrases can certainly be used on their own to decrease self-criticism and to promote mental health, just as walking an hour a day is good for your physical health even without the complementary practices of weightlifting or eating an extremely healthy diet.

Core Exercise

To practice lovingkindness, find a comfortable position as you practice the silent repetition of phrases wishing yourself (and/or others and all beings) well. If you like, you can match the phrases to a full breath (inhale and exhale) for each phrase. The following phrases are commonly used, although there are many variations.

Phrases

> May I be safe.
> May I be happy.
> May I be healthy.
> May I live with ease.

You can consider a range of alternative phrases, such as:

> May I be calm.
> May I be peaceful.
> May I be joyful.
> May I feel connected to other people and to the world.
> May my actions be skillful and kind.
> May I be healthy and strong.

Sequence

Your options are to either start by directing the phrases toward yourself and to proceed in the traditional manner outlined below, or to start with a benefactor and then move to yourself once you've connected with the feeling of loving-kindness toward another.

You can focus your LKM practice session on one of the categories (for instance, only on yourself or only toward the benefactor), and continue to practice that way for several days, weeks, or months before moving on to another category. Or, you can move through all of the categories in a single practice session, spending at least a few minutes on each category. Here is the traditional sequence in which to practice LKM:

Toward yourself (e.g., "May I be happy.")
Toward a "benefactor" or someone who has helped you
    (e.g., "May he/ she/ they be safe.")
Toward someone "neutral," someone you don't know or
    about whom you don't feel strongly
Toward someone "difficult," but remembering not to
    begin with the most "difficult" people in life
Toward all beings, excluding none (e.g., "May all be-
    ings be safe.")

Tips for Beginning LKM

The instructions above should be sufficient for you to give LKM a try, but as with any meditation practice, there are lots of nuances to explore and unfold. Here are more tips to help you get started with the practice.

ADOPT AN ATTITUDE OF
GENTLE EXPERIMENTATION

You can try LKM out and most likely benefit from it, even if it feels very odd at first. In fact, you might pause for a moment to give yourself permission to really try something new and different, beyond what is comfortable and familiar. You can bring a spirit of willing experimentation, as you might try out a few slight variations to find a routine that's at least ten minutes long at first, and that seems right to you. If you feel skeptical, that's okay.

EXPECT SOME CHALLENGES

If you're used to criticizing yourself, training in the other direction probably won't feel easy. It might be quite difficult at first. I encourage you not to give up because it seems hard or because you don't notice immediate changes. You will almost certainly have distractions: thoughts, memories, doubts, annoyances, plans for your next meal. Remember that LKM is a concentration practice. Cultivating the skill of managing distractions efficiently without becoming swept up in them is extremely useful—both for managing self-criticism and other unwanted thoughts. The idea is to notice any thoughts, memories, or reactions softly, without self-judgment, without overidentifying with them, and without getting lost in them. Return your focus—again and again and again and again. Keep it up.

CHOOSE YOUR PHRASES

There are many different phrases to use for LKM. You can try out the ones mentioned in this chapter, or survey those offered by other mindfulness teachers. Some of them won't seem right to you, some may resonate more strongly, and perhaps you'll find a few that feel just right. It's also completely fine to create your own phrases. You might ask yourself what you feel that you need in this point in your life (for instance, health, confidence, or connection), and to let those needs help you determine which phrases to use. The friendly wishes should be ones that promote a sense of enduring happiness or comfort, rather than more transitory hopes about a particular event, because the intention is to cultivate a stable sense of friendliness.[6]

PRACTICE SEVERAL TIMES A WEEK, OR EVERY DAY IF POSSIBLE

The power of LKM lies in the repetition of the phrases within each practice session and over the days and weeks of practice. The mindfulness teacher Sharon Salzberg recounts that she began this practice with an intensive week of concentrated meditation, wishing herself well using specific LKM phrases, and feeling "absolutely nothing." At the end of the week, she dropped a jar and it shattered, and her first thought was, "You are such a klutz, but I love you." She then thought, "Wow, look at that! Something did happen in this week of practice." Salzberg reflected, "All those hours, all those phrases where I was just dry and mechanical and I felt like nothing was happening. It was happening."[7]

DETERMINE THE ORDER OF RECIPIENTS FOR YOUR LKM MEDITATION

It's traditional to start with yourself (for instance, "May I be safe; May I be happy; May I be healthy; May I live with ease") and then, after a period of practice (perhaps a few weeks), to move to a "benefactor," someone who has helped you and for whom it is easy to feel kindness and gratitude. After practicing LKM for that person for a few more weeks, you then move to a neutral person. A neutral person is someone for whom you don't have very strong feelings, one way or the other. Perhaps it's a person who works at a coffee shop or the neighbor you barely know. In classroom settings, I've invited students to take a moment to wish the students around them good luck during the upcoming finals week. One student observed that "it felt great to send goodwill toward classmates I barely knew."

After you feel that you've generated a good measure of friendliness for that person, you could next focus your LKM on a "difficult" person. When you are beginning LKM, it's wise not to start with the person who has been the most difficult in your entire life. There are probably plenty of people about whom you feel mild unease or annoyance, and you can start with one of them. Finally, you would move on to practicing LKM for all beings, everywhere. Many practitioners elaborate with different categories of beings (e.g., known and unknown, seen and unseen, near or distant).

If you have immense difficulty starting LKM with a focus on yourself—if the idea of sending yourself good wishes feels just too weird or selfish—you don't have to practice that way. One of my students noted that "I feel slightly less authentic and more like I'm saying it because I have to. This is interesting because I obviously believe all of these things for others but giving myself the same level of understanding is trickier." If it seems more comfortable, you can start with the "benefactor" or someone for whom it's easy for you to send thoughts of goodwill.

Then, you can keep the feeling going but redirect it toward yourself as you move to LKM practice toward yourself. Over time, LKM practice can even soften those sorts of self-other distinctions. It creates a scope of friendliness that encompasses all beings, with all of their flaws, including you, including me, including everyone, everywhere.

In a single session of LKM practice, you can either call to mind one specific individual or move through all of the categories, spending at least five minutes on every category.

However, it is helpful to choose your focus before you start a session; that is, to pick the recipient or sequence of recipients that seems right and stick with that plan. People enjoy practicing LKM in a number of ways. I have a friend, also a psychologist, a very loving and warm person, who decided to focus her LKM practice on herself for over a year, so that most of her sessions included the phrases only for herself. That is a fine and normal way to practice. Some teachers advise you to progress to the next category only after you have established a deep sense of friendliness for the preceding category.

INCORPORATE GENTLE VISUALIZING
AND BODILY AWARENESS

As you repeat the LKM phrases for other people, it can help to picture them in your mind. However, if visualizations don't help or come easily, you don't need to strive or to force them. LKM practice may also be accompanied by physical feelings of softness or warmth. The experience of wishing others well is sometimes described as a "radiating" practice, and you may feel sensations in your heart or chest. According to the Buddhist scholar and monk Analayo, the physical sensation of metta can emerge as a feeling of softness somewhere in the middle of the chest. Many teachers describe a sense of radiating metta outward. Analayo emphasizes that metta radiation is soft and gentle rather than a forceful feeling of pushing out toward the intended recipients.[8]

PRACTICE WITH TENDER PATIENCE

Sharon Salzberg advises, "Let your mind rest in the phrases. You can be aware of the phrases either with the breath or just in themselves—the focus of the attention is the phrases. Let your mind rest within them."[9] Salzberg elsewhere advises that your pacing should be gentle and easy, without rushing the phrases or saying them in a harsh way.

TRY LKM BY YOURSELF, WITH A TEACHER, IN COMMUNITY, OR AS YOU WALK

If you like, you can certainly use guided lovingkindness meditations, where you listen to a teacher's voice taking you through the steps. Guided LKM meditations of various lengths abound on the Internet, apps, and at in-person or virtual meditation centers. There are also group meetings all over the world, both in-person and virtually, where people practice LKM together. You can practice LKM "undercover" in a business meeting, on a bus, at a group or family meal, or in a classroom, by directing your LKM phrases to each person in turn.

One lovely way to practice is an LKM walk. As you start walking, you repeat the phrases for yourself. Then, as you encounter other beings on your walk (a person crosses the street in front of you; a bird flaps down onto the concrete), you direct a "round" of LKM phrases toward that being. Then back to yourself, and then back to others whom you encounter. One student described infusing LKM into regular walks:

> After implementing LKM, I started becoming more intentional in the conversations that I have in my head. For example, while I am on my walk I see that flowers are budding and the cherry blossoms around my neighborhood are blooming. While I look at them, I tell myself, "May I bud and bloom vibrantly." I love walking to the International District through the Danny Woo garden and as I pass by aunties, uncles, grandmas, and grandpas, I pass the same phrase onto them: "May you bud and bloom vibrantly today."

The Scientific Evidence That LKM Works

Research demonstrates a range of benefits for LKM, including increased feelings of connection with other people, less racism, and more concern for the environment. Whereas self-criticism is linked with a full range of mental health challenges, LKM seems to improve a number of mental health difficulties. LKM practice is linked with improvements in depression, anxiety, stress, anger, and post-traumatic stress disorder (PTSD).[10] LKM also seems to help people manage physical health challenges, including back pain[11] and pain related to breast cancer.[12]

With respect to self-criticism, participants' reports of self-critical experiences were significantly reduced in a number of high-quality research studies examining the impact of three to seven weeks of LKM practice.[13] In fact, the studies that followed participants three months after their group LKM sessions had ended observed that their improvements in self-criticism and mental health were maintained.[14]

Other research has looked deeper to investigate how and why LKM seems to improve mental health. LKM seems to lead a range of positive responses in the brain and body, including the ability to regulate emotions.[15] For instance, LKM may help people calm down by reducing their heart rate and increasing activity in the parasympathetic nervous system.[16] Another mechanism of action has to do with the default mode network (DMN), discussed earlier in the introduction and in chapter 3. Because LKM practice can decrease activation of the default mode network[17]—the habitual, repetitive patterns of thought related to self-criticism—it may promote well-being by engaging healthier mental processes.

In 2018, Suzanne B. Johnson, a researcher at Georgia State University, and her colleagues wondered how a six-session intervention that combined mindfulness, LKM, and compassion practice might reduce depression in fifty-nine low-income African American men and women who had recently attempted suicide. They randomized individuals to either participate in the compassion meditation group (including LKM) or to take part in a six-session support group. After the six sessions, the participants in the compassion meditation group reported larger reductions in self-criticism than those who had attended the support group. The researchers analyzed the data to further determine that the change in self-criticism explained the change in depression. That is, it was common for participants to first become less self-critical and then to experience less depression as a result.[18]

LKM seems to work by building a range of resources over a period of several weeks. Participants who took part in a seven-week LKM group reported increases in positive emotions, which then led to higher levels of self-acceptance, social support, positive relationships with other people, and mindfulness. After those resources became stronger, people reported fewer symptoms of depression and increased life satisfaction. Those "resource gains" from LKM practice were maintained when the researchers measured them again, fifteen months after the original study period.[19]

LKM seems to generate positive emotions toward other people.[20] The University of Sussex researchers Alexander Stell and Tom Farsides point out that most positive emotions have to do with attention toward yourself, but that LKM focuses positive emotions outward, toward other people.[21] For those of us who struggle with self-criticism, it can be a relief to shift some of our attention away from judging ourselves and toward kindly regarding other people. LKM practice seems to decrease focus on yourself.[22]

LKM can also shift the experience of being angry. People who engaged in LKM described feeling relief from their anger after the practice: they explained that they were able to regard the people who had angered them as multifaceted individuals who were also affected by a range of complex and difficult circumstances, motives, and feelings.[23] One teacher reflected that "my mind often spins out into considering how I've been wronged, replaying the situation over and over again, getting further enraged, and then by introducing lovingkindness—it's like a balm or a salve to all of it. It pretty quickly douses the fire in my mind."[24]

LKM appears to help individuals feel more connected to other people and more positive about them. Even a single session of LKM has been shown to increase feelings of social connection, on both conscious and more implicit levels.[25] Several studies have observed that practicing LKM decreases racial prejudice.[26] Other studies note that LKM interventions have reduced implicit bias against stigmatized individuals and increased more positive attitudes toward them, including Black individuals, people who use substances, and homeless individuals.[27] After six to eight weeks of LKM training, researchers observe higher levels of empathy for others and improved communication skills.[28]

My students' reports of how LKM affects their attitudes and behaviors toward other people parallels many of these research findings. One student noted that, "I felt myself having more positive feelings toward strangers, like the man who works at the gas station. Normally I would go in there and get my things and leave, but then I started asking how his day was going, getting to know him, and wishing him a good day at the end of every conversation." Another student noticed being kinder to a roommate with whom they had struggled to get along. During the pandemic, another student began to practice LKM after a long period of isolation and depression. After some time with the practice, the student noted that "I gradually opened my closed heart and started to socialize with my classmates and neighbors. This process made me gradually feel that my body and mind became healthier."

It remains to be determined to what extent LKM and similar practices actually result in more desirable actions toward other people and the world. At this point, some scholars review the available literature and conclude that LKM and other meditation practices have a generally positive but limited contribution to beneficial actions toward others,[29] whereas others survey the literature with more certainty about a link between LKM practice and compassionate behavior.[30] Some of the observed links between LKM practice and actual beneficial action include research demonstrating that LKM can enhance pro-environmental attitudes and environmental decision-making,[31] as well as the research that LKM can improve communication skills.[32] If you begin to practice LKM yourself, you might notice not only whether it changes your self-criticism but also if it impacts how you relate to other people and to the wider world.

Obstacles to LKM

In addition to the initial skepticism that people commonly report when first learning about LKM or practicing it, some people feel selfish in wishing themselves well, or unworthy of kind wishes. If those feelings arise, you can notice them gently and still give LKM a good try. Remember that those feelings reflect mental conditioning. They are not the truth. People all over the world are practicing LKM and including you ("May all beings be happy") in their good wishes. LKM isn't a judgment—it isn't a screening process to select whether or not someone is worthy or unworthy of good wishes. It's a practice of wishing everyone well, even the "worst" beings, full stop. It doesn't mean that everyone is perfect, or that difficult characteristics and harmful actions don't matter, or that you need to accept or disregard the real problems that exist. You can let those challenges be there, including the problems that you perceive within yourself, and still wish yourself and others well.

It might feel extremely uncomfortable to wish yourself well. It could actually feel unpleasant, wrong, disgusting, or even emerge as physical aches and pains. When people who have experienced a lot of personal difficulties (especially having been mistreated, abused, or neglected) have a negative response to practicing friendliness or compassion, that reaction is sometimes called "backdraft." The term is a metaphor, relating one's mind state to an oxygen-depleted fire worsening once it is suddenly exposed to fresh air.[33] "Backdraft" can lead people to abandon LKM, which is understandable, because the practice might feel actively unpleasant. But returning to the status quo maintains self-critical anguish and related mental health challenges. It can be helpful to label "backdraft" with the word and to know that you aren't alone if such feelings occur. Often beneath the discomfort of LKM there is grief: the ache of having been deprived of deep friendliness and unconditional love for so long. If you can be patient with the discomfort, anger, grief, aches, and sorrow of "backdraft," and treat those feelings with friendliness as well, they can abate.

Another obstacle some people encounter is feeling as though they don't really have the capacity or energy to wish other people well. Perhaps you doubt whether you can truly care for other people, or for all beings. If you're in great pain, it might feel too difficult to imagine caring for others, or even for yourself. Perhaps you can allow those ideas or feelings to be present even as you put forth the effort to practice LKM. "From the point of view of the Buddhist teaching," explains Sharon Salzberg, "we all have that capacity to love. No experience of suffering, of loneliness or of unlovability we may have gone through or may yet go through can ever destroy that capacity. And that faith is the bedrock of lovingkindness."[34]

You may feel uncomfortable wishing yourself well. All too often, taking care of yourself or other people seems like a zero-sum game: either the energy or resources go toward your needs, or toward theirs. One LKM beginner wondered, "Am I wrong to put 'I' first before anyone else in the world?"[35] However, the idea of starting with practicing LKM toward yourself isn't to choose friendliness for yourself over friendliness for others. It is meant to ground yourself in the lived, moment-to-moment sensation of friendly feelings, experienced both as emanating from within yourself and as receiving the good feelings that you direct toward yourself. Practicing LKM can thereby lead you to become a stronger source of friendliness toward yourself and toward all beings. As one of my students reflected, "LKM specifically encourages me to designate the same amount of care and time to myself as I do to others and acts as a buffer against my self-deprecating tendencies." That description conveys LKM's balancing effect on attention and care: everyone is included, and there are enough kind feelings to go around without any need to leave yourself out.

You might think that when you practice LKM, you need to suppress difficult feelings, like jealousy, anger, or pain. You don't. The compassionate perspective that LKM aims to cultivate is all-inclusive. The teacher Ajahn Sumedho asserts that in LKM practice, "nothing is left out." If challenging feelings arise, try to notice them without identifying with them—even if they are very strong, even if they seem to mean something about you, or even if they trigger a cascade of stories and memories. It can help to direct your friendliness toward difficult feelings and to yourself as you feel them. Ajahn Sumedho advises that "having *metta* for our own moods, our own emotional habits, enables us to let them be what they are, to neither indulge in them nor to reject them, but to recognize, 'This is my mood. This is how it feels.' The attitude is one of patience, nonaversion, and kindness."[36] Relating to difficult feelings is not a diversion but rather a fundamental part of LKM practice.

You might feel bored with the practice, or it might seem as though no changes are taking place. As with all types of meditation, this is par for the course. One student noticed that "it felt almost like a 'fake it until you make it' situation before any changes were evident." You will most likely be distracted. One teacher who recently started LKM described being "easily distracted by my floating thoughts."[37] It takes lots of practice to handle distractions calmly and to return quickly to your focus. You build your focusing skills by noticing you've become distracted, returning your focus gently, and by doing that hundreds of times, on purpose.

A few months into my practice, I noticed that part of my brain was repeating LKM phrases, and another part was off daydreaming, thinking about this and that. I then started to notice that this happened frequently. Attention is complicated.

Many meditation practices are designed to develop self-control over attention. I could certainly get frustrated or even berate myself for becoming distracted. However, the instruction for LKM is to hold your attention on the phrases gently—not to act as a mean taskmaster, and not to feel scared or stressed about losing focus. You could imagine holding your attention as a bouquet of flowers, or perhaps a water balloon. If you drop your attention, you pick it up. But don't hold your attention so tightly that your effort crushes it.

When you get to the "difficult" person, you might notice feelings of frustration, guilt, disappointment, or exhaustion. One student noted, "I was a little taken aback by the thoughts and resistance that came to mind when sending positive energy to some people." People sometimes observe physical sensations of tightness or contraction when repeating LKM phrases for "difficult" people. You might find it impossible to generate any positive feelings. This is a good opportunity to be patient with yourself and to observe your experience gently. You don't have to feel anything in particular at any given moment. Rather, the goal is to make the effort of repeating the phrases for different individuals or categories of beings.

LKM and Affirmations

Is LKM the same as practicing affirmations? Well, it depends what is meant by "affirmations." LKM phrases do affirm some of your deepest hopes for yourself, for other people, and for the world. They might not reflect exactly how you feel in this moment, but they are intended to reflect how you want to feel, and what is important to you. However, practicing LKM isn't the same as making affirmations in the general sense of the word—that is, they're not statements about how wonderful you are, reminders of your personal strengths, or expressions of a belief that anything in particular is going to happen. LKM phrases are meant to deepen a particular attitude of wishing oneself and others well. It may seem simplistic, but the data show that activating those well-wishes over and over leads to powerful results in terms of self-talk and well-being.

Practicing "affirmations" usually means silently repeating positive phrases that are intended to help contradict self-criticism and negative thoughts (for example, "I am successful," or "I am loved"). There are thousands of suggested "positive affirmations" out there, but very little actual scientific evidence to indicate that those types of affirmations are effective. When I investigated the evidence to determine whether "positive affirmations" are beneficial, the only research study I found that showed a potential link between positive affirmations and well-being was rather vague about what kinds of statements people might be using.[38] Studies of "affirmations" in the psychological literature use the term to describe a range of different concepts, including self-enhancement, tuning in to personal strengths, and clarifying values.

"Self-enhancement," or the tendency to interpret experiences and information in a way that is flattering toward yourself, seems like it could help diminish self-criticism, but it is also linked with higher levels of narcissism, ego involvement, biased thinking, and with lower self-esteem and diminished well-being.[39] Over the course of their college careers, "self-enhancers" showed reductions in their self-esteem and in well-being. Imagine that you have a tendency to interpret most things as meaning something positive about yourself, but then you fail a class or a partner breaks up with you. Self-enhancement doesn't work well when things get hard; other cognitive styles (for instance, a growth mindset) are more useful when times are tough. LKM is a more resilient approach to handling difficulties than self-enhancement affirmations, because LKM phrases do not involve building yourself up but rather cultivating a sense of friendliness in any circumstance. For instance, one student noticed that LKM practice helped assuage disappointment:

> A day I remember that I realized that this practice was helping me was when I had thrown in a scrimmage and didn't do as well as I hoped, I didn't get stressed and upset, instead saying to a teammate "It's all good, man, at least I got tomorrow." It was a moment where I surprised myself, but also something that allowed me to move on with peace of mind.

Whereas self-enhancement has some notable drawbacks, the practice of tuning in to strengths and values can be beneficial, either through LKM practice or otherwise.[40] In fact, people sometimes note that LKM helps them connect with their values. One person observed, "As soon as I first read the words, I felt like I was coming home to my truer self, the one who does try to cultivate an unconditional love toward other people, and which can be masked by challenges of life, and frustrations with other people."[41] Similarly, one of my students reflected, "I feel like I'm more in touch with my deeper purpose and values when I spend time meditating in general, and lovingkindness brings this to a new level."

LKM and Prayer

Prayer is a complex set of practices, some of which share attributes with LKM and some of which do not. Among other things, prayer can reflect praise, worship, or adoration toward the Divine; the idea of "drawing near" or connecting with the Divine; apologies or supplication; and petitions, intercessions, or requests for different kinds of help. In both LKM and prayer, a person connects with their deepest values, and puts effort into developing their mind and heart in a particular direction and on purpose. Like LKM, prayer might include specific words, phrases, or longer texts that are meaningful, or that someone repeats several times.

In Western secular settings, LKM often focuses cultivating your own kind feelings rather than connecting with a divine presence or asking for specific outcomes. If you use the format, "May I be safe," the "may I" part could be confusing. It might sound like an entreaty. But the "may I" isn't meant to ask, "Please can I be safe?" but rather to incline your mind and heart toward your own good wishes. You don't have to use the "may I be safe" format if the "may I" seems strange to you. You could say, "I hope that all beings are safe," or "I wish for all beings to be safe." Instead of worrying about whether or not the good wishes ever come to pass, LKM is a training system that is meant to condition your own inner kindness right in this moment, and again in this moment now, and again in this moment now, throughout your practice.

Some people decide to integrate mindfulness practices, including LKM, into their prayers. If you would like to do that, you certainly can. For instance, many Jewish and Christian people want to adhere to the Old Testament commandment to "Love thy neighbor as thyself" (Leviticus 19:18) and/ or to the New Testament commandment to "Love one another" (John 13:34 and John 15:17), but they wonder how to develop love for others that they don't seem to feel. In fact, some interpretations of the phrase, found in both the Old Testament and the New Testament, "Love thy neighbor as thyself" (Matthew 22:39) view the phrase as including an order that you should, in fact, love yourself (the biblical quote certainly doesn't mean that you should love your neighbor in a minimal or conditional way, even if your love toward yourself feels limited or nonexistent). Non-Buddhists, including Christian and Jewish people, have reported that practicing LKM phrases enhances spiritual feelings of love toward themselves and others—and that they incorporate LKM or other phrases into their religious practice.

One of my students described implementing the idea of LKM phrases into Christian prayer. The intention of cultivating specific qualities of mind is present, as are the features of repeating and concentrating on the chosen phrases during a specific period of meditation:

> The phrases I would choose would be Scripture verses that hold a truth about myself that I want to penetrate deeper inside. For example, I tried "For God has not given us a spirit of fear, but of power and of love and of a sound mind" (2 Timothy 1:7). In going through the steps of the practice in repetition and meditation, I really felt these truths sink deeper in. As I tried it a couple times with the traditional phrases such as "May I live in safety," I felt the same to be true then as well. I simply enjoyed doing it with Bible verses more as it resonates personally with me more and I believe it to have power and life.

LKM as a Form of Mantra Meditation

A *mantra* (from the Sanskrit, sometimes translated as "mind instrument"[42]) means any repeated sound, word, or phrase, often used with the intention of cultivating a particular mindset, feeling, or aspect of consciousness. You can say the word or phrase out loud, chant it, or simply repeat it silently in your mind. The idea is that you become quite connected with the word, so that it infuses your mind and becomes a kind of mental landmark or a mental "home" where your thoughts can rest.

Mantra meditation is a type of concentration meditation, in which you try to focus on the sound, word, or phrase that you have selected. When your attention departs from your focus, the idea is to notice that departure and then to begin again, with as little drama or criticism as possible about the interruption.

Based on these descriptions, LKM can be considered a form of mantra (or "mantram") meditation. And indeed, the vast majority of scientific research about the effects of mantra meditation involves LKM, and many of those studies are described above. There are, however, some published studies that investigate mantra meditations more generally. Benefits from repeating or listening to mantras include reductions in stress and anxiety,[43] fewer post-traumatic stress symptoms,[44] and improvements in well-being and quality of life.[45]

Why does mantra meditation work? It's a form of concentration meditation, not so different from focusing on your breathing. It's just that here the object of focus is the sound, word, or phrase instead of the breath. The benefits of learning to manage attention and not to identify with distractions are most likely the same, whether your focus is the breath or a mantra. In both cases, you're training your mind away from its default way of thinking (reflecting the brain's "default mode network" and the habit of self-criticism) and engaging the "task positive" brain network that is linked with more intentional focus and greater well-being.

LKM at Work

Most people spend a large portion of their waking hours at work, with its many challenges and frustrations. You might struggle with your own concentration or productivity. Difficult feelings about other people—customers, patients, leaders, or colleagues—will almost certainly arise. Criticism on all sides is common: your own criticism about yourself, others, or the job, as well as others' criticism, either real or imagined. LKM can shake things up a bit at work, in a good way. For instance, LKM practice has been linked with greater well-being and lower levels of stress among flight attendants,[46] student teachers,[47] and health professionals.[48]

There was a time in my life when my job included a ninety-minute weekly departmental meeting that I dreaded. I decided that I would use the time to practice my loving-kindness phrases for myself ("May I be safe. May I be happy. May I be healthy. May I live with ease") in my head during the meeting, over and over. I didn't resent the time that the meeting took because I had already chosen to use that time for LKM practice. I don't think that I was any more distracted during the meetings than before I started the strategy. Who isn't thinking about other things (self-judgment, judging others, emails, lunch) during a meeting? With my new LKM initiative, I actually felt more grounded and present because I had an anchor for my attention.

Teachers who practiced LKM over three weeks found that although they had been accustomed to blaming themselves during challenging situations in the classroom, they started to refrain from harsh self-criticism. They described less of a sense of striving or a need to be perfect, and a decreased need to control classroom tasks. Teachers reported using LKM to accept and manage anxiety and other challenging emotions. They also noted improvements in their ability to tolerate conflict and to remain calm when students did not meet their expectations. One teacher observed that "I felt I was more patient, relaxed, and overall more effective with everyone I had to deal with at school." Another teacher found that the practice shifted their sense of purpose in the classroom: "I have become aware that a good teacher is not necessarily the most knowledgeable one but the one who is fully present to students."[49]

Teachers also reported initiating more effective interactions with students. For example, one teacher noted that his intentions of lovingkindness, cultivated during LKM practice, did not match his urge to remove difficult students from the classroom. He observed that "my feelings of anger and frustration toward these students contradicted the verses of the actual meditation that I had been trying to recite." He found himself instead searching for strategies (for example, making a new seating plan, or speaking to students or their parents privately) that could be more inclusive and helpful, rather than resorting to eliminating difficult students from the classroom.[50]

There are also interesting reports from healthcare workers who use LKM. After ten weeks of implementing LKM and related practices, healthcare workers reported lower levels of burnout, stress, and anxiety, increased joy at work, and greater abilities to regulate emotions.[51] The Zen teacher Lewis Richmond described working with "Christine," a nurse who reported that the feeling of not having enough time was the hardest part of her job. Christine decided to try repeating the phrases "plenty of time, plenty of care" to tune in to her deepest values. Since she didn't have time at work for seated practice, she repeated the phrases silently as she walked the halls of the hospital.

Christine said that at first, repeating the phrases seemed artificial and rote. She then infused a feeling into her practice rather than simply repeating the phrases. She recalled caring for her most captivating patient, "Princess Juliana," a woman with royal heritage who was "gracious and charming," who thanked Christine for everything that she did. After some period of repeating "plenty of time, plenty of care" with Juliana in mind, Christine began to feel a bit better about her work. A few months later, she reported that she had kept the practice up for a while, but then she got tired of it. She reflected that doing the practice for a time had really benefited her, but that it had evolved into something else: "When I walk down the halls, I kind of hum inside my mind and try to keep a certain feeling in my heart. It's hard to describe, but it really seems to help. I feel like I'm managing the chaos, instead of letting it get to me." She also reported that she had begun sitting down with patients who were having problems, because she remembered Princess Juliana telling her to "Sit down, dear."

The story illustrates a few themes, including the importance of practicing in a way that reflects your individual preferences and feelings and the value of trying out different variations in practice. Richmond writes, "Christine had taken what began as a gateway practice to a deeper level. . . . In bringing a spiritual practice to life, it is important to carry the effort lightly. It is all too easy to turn the effort into a kind of homework assignment or chore."[52]

Of course, there are many truly terrible work situations for which LKM is an insufficient remedy. If you are being chronically overworked, harassed, or put in unsafe situations, it's important to take action. But LKM can help assuage work-related criticism toward oneself or others, and it might even help you clarify which areas call for direct action and which might benefit from reframing your own attitudes.

Spontaneous LKM

As noted above, using LKM to build feelings of friendliness requires actual practice sessions, or periods of "formal meditation," in which you decide that you will repeat the phrases for several minutes at a time. After a while, you might notice that the phrases or related feelings arise outside of formal meditation. Marvelous! After all, the idea isn't to become a superstar at LKM during the minutes that you're practicing but to build your overall friendliness and well-being, and to reduce your self-criticism and distressing feelings in general.

During the period of writing this chapter, I had moments of spontaneous, LKM-inspired friendly wishes. In one instance, I was walking on the sidewalk, beneath a construction site, underneath the wooden boards and metal poles of scaffolding. Metal clanged, saws buzzed, jackhammers roared. The thought arose, "What if this scaffolding collapses and I get hurt?" I decided to send wishes for safety and happiness to the construction workers above me. My fear calmed. It became a smaller part of my experience as a feeling of warmth and contentment became my primary sensation. It happened again in traffic ("Am I headed the right way? What's the holdup over there?"), where my stress eased as I directed

friendly thoughts ("I hope you have a good rest of your day!")
to the other drivers around me. And most surprisingly to me,
when I was in a relatively neutral mood, I went to take out
the compost bin and a bird flapped down a few feet in front
of me. I looked at the bird. I wished that the bird would have
a truly fabulous day of being a bird. My task—taking out
the garbage—was transformed into a totally different experience. I felt joy and just delight as I turned and walked back
up the steps and into my front door.

Whether you have experienced spontaneous moments of
wishing lovingkindness or not, you can be on the lookout
for real-world opportunities to practice LKM. A bus, train,
airplane, class, or meeting can be a lovely opportunity. You
might set the intention to practice LKM anytime you're waiting in line, or silently repeat LKM phrases at a coffee shop
or grocery store. You could also decide that you will practice
LKM during moments of hardship or frustration (although
I would recommend this as a complementary LKM practice
rather than a primary one, because cultivating LKM requires a focused energy that is more challenging to access
in moments of difficulty). You can also let friendliness arise
spontaneously, in regular, everyday life, and gently observe
the benefits that arise after a sustained effort of intentional
practice.

LKM is a practice meant to connect us with our own inherent
goodness. If you struggle with self-criticism, the idea that
you are inherently good, lovable, and loving might be hard
to imagine. When you feel self-critical or unworthy, you can
notice those feelings in a caring way, just as you might tend
a cut or a scrape on a child in your care. You might try tell-

ing yourself that many aspects of self-criticism reflect conditioned beliefs that stem from difficult experiences, rather than the truth of who you are or all that you might become. Relating to yourself and to others in a friendlier manner doesn't negate any harm that was done in the past, but it can reduce the likelihood of further harm, including the inner harm of self-criticism.

I wish you well as you consider or continue LKM. I know it might seem daunting, or you might not feel particularly confident about it. In US culture, we often think of confidence as knowing that you're already good at something. With LKM and similar techniques, confidence is more about having faith in the techniques themselves and in your own ability to grow new capacities. When you're self-critical, it can be easy to think that you can't ever learn to do things differently, that change is impossible. You might take heart from the scientific evidence demonstrating that LKM is an effective path for reducing self-criticism and troubling mental health symptoms. Perhaps you admire other people or teachers who have benefited from LKM or similar practices. You might remember that self-doubt is a common feature on the road to becoming more confident. The Buddha said (presumably to monks who doubted their own abilities): "One *can* cultivate the good. If it were not possible, I would not ask you to do it." May befriending yourself, either through LKM or another strategy, unfold well, in a way that soothes self-criticism and related suffering.

May you be safe.

May you be happy.

May you be healthy.

May your life unfold with ease.

REFLECTION QUESTIONS

1. What is your initial reaction to the idea of training friendliness (practicing lovingkindness meditation, or LKM)? If you practice several minutes of LKM, how do you feel afterward? Are your initial reaction and post-practice response similar, or do they differ?

2. Do you have a default way of relating to strangers? For instance, avoiding eye contact, or critiquing their outfits or bodies?

3. If you think about practicing LKM, is there an order for the "targets" that seems right to you? For instance, some people practice LKM for themselves ("May I be safe. May I be happy. May I be healthy. May I live with ease.") for months or years before trying LKM for other people. Other people feel awkward or selfish sending themselves kind wishes and find that it's easier to start practicing LKM with a friend, family member, or mentor in mind. What seems right for you as you start or continue your LKM practice?

4. Which LKM phrases seem like the best fit for you at this time?

5. If you tried to practice LKM, did any difficult thoughts, feelings, or memories arise, or experiences that seemed like obstacles to your practice (such as distraction, boredom, discomfort, or annoyance)? Were you able to relate kindly and gently to those experiences?

6. After practicing LKM for a period of a few weeks, what do you notice? Has the experience of practicing varied or changed over time? Have you noticed yourself relating differently to your own experiences, or to other people, even outside of your specific moments of LKM practice?

6

Allowing All Feelings, Skillfully

THIS MORNING I woke from a bad dream feeling groggy, downhearted, and just rather "off." The dream took place at a movie theater, where some college friends had ignored me and excluded me from sitting with them, including someone with whom I had once felt extremely close but who had ended our relationship abruptly decades ago. As I awoke more fully, I considered ignoring the internal residue from the dream and just getting on with the morning: writing some emails, showering, and starting the laundry before the kids got up. But I sensed that I would have an emotional hangover that would permeate my day in subtle ways: worsening my interactions with my family, coloring my mood, and draining my energy.

Instead of ignoring my feelings related to the dream, I sat down with the intention of allowing myself to feel them and to treat them with attention and care. First, I tried to tune in to my breathing to connect with whatever was going on inside in this very moment. Next, I posed the question, "What feelings are here?" I couldn't quite notice anything besides a general ache, perhaps related to sadness, rejection, confusion, and betrayal. I then asked myself, "These feelings that I'm noticing, and my overall unease from the dream—where do I feel these things in my body?" Well, the top of my neck seemed tight, as did the muscles in my forehead and around my eyes. As I breathed, I felt patches of tension throughout my chest. I stayed with my goal of noticing my emotional and physical sensations for a few minutes in an open and friendly way. What came next surprised me. I observed myself feeling not only the grief and surprise related to suddenly losing a close relationship but also feeling the joy and intimacy that had once characterized it and that had made its loss so painful. Those feelings were real as well. I noticed sensations connected to the whole array of emotions for another couple of minutes. The muscles in my neck and forehead seemed to release some of their tension, and my chest felt softer and lighter, tender instead of tight. I reflected that those five or ten minutes of allowing all feelings had been well worth it. I felt more settled and balanced, as though the range of painful and loving feelings had been integrated into a larger picture. All in all, I ended the practice in a much better state of mind.

In the preceding chapters, I have described a range of strategies to build new self-talk habits that are friendly, kind, and encouraging. But even though those strategies can decrease self-criticism and improve well-being, they can't prevent all of the painful experiences that are an inherent part of being human. Even without the challenge of self-criticism, we will all face some rough times.

I saved this chapter for last because it describes strategies that might not seem as uplifting at first glance. These practices involve tuning in to painful feelings, because recognizing the truth of what is happening is often necessary to address it effectively. When you allow yourself to feel a full range of emotions, you also gain the opportunity to apply your own support and encouragement to inner realms that deeply need it. The practices in this chapter provide specific frameworks for you to access and care for difficult feelings in the moment without becoming overwhelmed by them. They also build capacities that can replace patterns such as numbing painful feelings, becoming lost in your thoughts and feelings, or criticizing yourself for your emotions or the way that you're handling them.

Allowing all feelings doesn't mean that you have to act upon difficult feelings, or even to prioritize giving them more attention than other types of experiences. Instead, allowing all feelings refers to acknowledging your feelings with attention and care. It's meant to provide some relief from patterns of either constricting the emotions that you experience or getting stuck in painful feelings and what they might mean about you. In this chapter, we'll experiment with allowing all feelings to be there, using practices that can help you feel safe, supported, and comforted.

———

"Allowing all feelings, skillfully" contrasts with two common but problematic emotional styles. One style involves allowing only a few feelings while restricting, numbing, suppressing, or distracting yourself from most feelings (for instance, deciding that you're not going to be sad about a breakup, and making yourself really busy with work instead). Another style involves experiencing a great many feelings and thoughts about feelings, but doing so *unskillfully* (for example, ruminating about the breakup by imagining "what ifs" or hypothetical conversations that lead to new levels of sadness and anger). It's tricky, because it can seem like you're being very open and in touch with your feelings, when you're actually lost in thoughts and feelings about your feelings and perhaps overly identified with your own feelings. Aspects of both styles can be present within the same person, and both styles can also include self-criticism about feelings. And all of these tendencies (allowing few feelings, allowing feelings and thoughts about feelings but doing so unskillfully, and self-criticism) are linked with lower levels of well-being.

"Allowing all feelings, skillfully" involves practicing a particular way of relating to your feelings. It means neither pushing away your feelings nor letting them run the show. It reflects a sense of witnessing your feelings, an awareness that extends beyond the particular feelings themselves. It includes practicing kindness and patience toward yourself when difficult feelings arise. It reflects refraining from self-criticism about your feelings. Finally, it prioritizes present-moment sensations rather than thoughts, feelings, memories, or plans related to the feelings.

There are at least three specific techniques (the self-compassion break; the RAIN technique of recognizing feelings, allowing them to exist, showing interest in them, and not identifying with them; and breathing meditation) that build the capacity of allowing feelings skillfully. Remember, it's the consistent practice of new habits, rather than reading and agreeing with certain perspectives, that creates real change. I'll describe each practice in turn in this chapter. First, however, it might be helpful to observe your current habits of restricting feelings, ruminating about feelings, or criticizing your feelings.

Restricting Feelings

"Suck it up, Buttercup!" "Man up!" "Pull yourself up by your bootstraps." I've heard many people confide that they speak to themselves this way during difficult moments. I get it. It's normal to want painful emotions to disappear so that you can get on with your life. In the rush of wanting everything to feel better—even our self-talk—it's common to ignore or minimize pain. Or, you might believe that you don't have time or room in your life to feel your feelings or as though you don't want to give another person the (imagined) satisfaction of having an emotional response to their behavior. It's also typical to allow yourself to experience some feelings but not others. Some feelings might feel easier, more familiar, or more acceptable, or perhaps they fit more with how you see yourself or what others expect from you. But only allowing some feelings, either consciously or unconsciously, is problematic. Attempts to prevent difficult feelings don't actually work very well, but trying to ignore them might take some of your energy, and also numb your ability to notice feelings in general, including more positive ones.

When restricting your feelings doesn't work (that is, you still feel the way that you feel, even though you don't think that you should), you might then criticize yourself for having unwanted emotions or for not handling them "well enough." Then, you're left with both the painful emotions (in fact, they probably feel even more terrible) plus feelings of failure and agitation when the painful feelings persist.

In the short term, distracting yourself or compartmentalizing pain might be useful. For instance, I remember a period of feeling upset about a difficult supervisor at work and tearing up about it during the subway ride home. Depending on how late I finished work and how many other commuters were on the train, there were some evenings when I stayed present with my feelings about my struggles at work, and other times when I chose to focus on staying alert to the scene around me until I could get home and let my emotions unfold. It's not uncommon that people need to push aside painful emotions to get their work done, or even to calm down a bit in order to handle a difficult situation wisely.

When you avoid painful feelings, they might actually become stronger. You might bottle up your annoyance toward your messy roommate for several weeks and then blow up at them one day when you've just had enough of being the only one who ever cleans out the refrigerator. And there's another important reason not to use distraction or suppression as your main coping strategy: if you don't practice actually handling difficult feelings, you can't build your capacity to manage them or boost your confidence that you can actually cope with them.

It's easy to fall into a cycle, consciously or unconsciously, of assuming that you can't manage your feelings, of then distracting yourself with your phone, with work, with socializing, or with drugs or food or alcohol, and therefore getting no practice actually navigating through the feelings, so that when the next rough patch comes, you feel incapable of handling it without the same kind of distraction. I don't mean to be confusing, because I really do think that some amount of distraction can be useful, especially when you choose it consciously and combine it with other strategies. ("I'm going to watch two episodes of my show on Netflix to help me calm down, then write in my journal about how I'm feeling, and then figure out what to say to my sister.")

Restricting feelings might prevent people from working

out necessary changes or growing new capacities. Suffering may be a signal that something in our lives or out in the world needs a different approach. Acknowledging pain is an important part of being a responsible person, friend, and citizen. A style of ignoring problems— from personal ones like destructive habits to societal ones like global warming and racism—can perpetuate them. Knowing that problems exist is a crucial step toward taking action.

People who practice new approaches to challenging feelings, including mindfulness meditation techniques, are often surprised at whole realms of feelings that emerge—not just "big" feelings, and not only painful feelings that might have been buried but smaller or more subtle sensations. It's common to cut ourselves off from feelings that seem kind of boring or not worth our attention. But then, we risk staying out of balance, a captive to the human "negativity bias" that draws our focus to what's most painful, while disregarding other feelings that are small, pleasant, or neutral.

Resisting Rumination

Allowing all feelings (skillfully) doesn't mean allowing all ruminations, judgments, and analysis. Often, I'll sit down to meditate, and my mind will start composing an email to someone. I can feel the tug of my mind striving to choose the right words. I might have emotions connected to the content of the email or about the intended recipient. In those moments, I do my best to pause and to redirect my attention back to my bodily sensations and emotions in the current moment. If I'm focused on choosing words or how I'm going to communicate my thoughts to another person, I'm not connecting with lived sensations of my own experience. I'm managing, fixing, doing. That has its time and place, but it isn't the practice of allowing all feelings, skillfully.

If you find yourself planning, getting lost in the complex history that contributed to your feelings, thinking repetitive thoughts about the feelings, or fixating on the past or the future, you can gently notice what's happening before redirecting your attention to the present-moment sensations and emotions that you feel in this very moment. Planning for the future and understanding the past can be very important, but when practicing the specific skill of allowing all feelings skillfully, they are a distraction. "Feel the feeling and drop the storyline," advises meditation teacher Susan Piver.[1]

Rumination can be misleading. When we think about our feelings, it can seem as though we're experiencing emotions deeply, or as though we're in the midst of developing greater insight. Perhaps you can gently question those assumptions. You might ask, "Am I in touch with my bodily, lived experience of my feeling in this moment—the immediate sensations of the feeling underneath all of these thoughts?" You might also ponder, "Am I truly in the midst of learning new material about this feeling or situation, or am I elaborating upon information that I already know, in a sort of repetitive way?" Buddhist psychology uses the term *near enemy* to refer to something that masquerades as a virtue but isn't. In that sense, rumination might be considered the near enemy of allowing all feelings, because it might seem like you are allowing everything to exist just as it is, but your mind is actually proliferating new interpretations and emotions about what's already there. Rumination can also reflect avoidance or self-protection; people can "intellectualize" or overanalyze their feelings to help guard themselves from actually feeling them.

The mindfulness teacher Joseph Goldstein describes "the wisdom of no," by explaining that "so often in spiritual practice we emphasize yes—the yes of acceptance, openness, richness, fullness of experience. And this yes is an effective antidote to the patterns of self-judgment, contraction, and limitation. But there is also the wisdom of no, when we recognize that some things are not skillful, not helpful, and not leading to happiness. At those times, we can practice saying, 'No thanks, I'll pass.'"[2]

The "wisdom of no" is particularly useful for avenues of thought that you've already been down. If you know why you feel a particular way, you don't need to reanalyze or relitigate it every time the feeling arises. You can also use the "wisdom of no" when you see yourself falling into habitual patterns about your feelings: criticizing them, suppressing them, thinking about your feelings and related factors repetitively (rumination), strategizing about how to change them, or overfocusing on the strongest feelings and missing subtle feelings.

Reducing Overidentification

Another facet of unskillfully allowing feelings is overidentification. Overidentification reflects confusion between *having* a feeling and assuming that you *are* the feeling. The Tibetan teacher Anyen Rinpoche noted that when he came to the United States, he was surprised at the amount of time that the people around him focused on their emotions, to the exclusion of the people and situations around them. He reflected that this focus seemed to make people unhappy. He also observes how the English language can reinforce overidentification with emotions. Anyen Rinpoche points out that in English we say, "I am angry," but that other languages might format the idea "I have anger" or, as he notes from the Tibetan language, "Anger is present."[3]

You can easily see how overidentification with feelings leads to self-criticism about feelings. If I *am* the emotions that I experience, I must be pretty crummy if I feel so many difficult emotions. This self-critical view about challenging emotions maintains them, because having a difficult feeling and then judging yourself as bad for having it leads to feeling even worse, which leaves you blaming yourself even more.

It can help to remember that difficult feelings arise outside of conscious choice, and that many painful feelings are normal reactions to stressful situations. A commonly repeated metaphor is that you are the sky, and your feelings are the weather. Observing your feelings as passing events, rather than as the essence of who you are, seems to make them stick less.

Self-Criticism about Feelings

Self-criticism about feelings can mask all kinds of assumptions, including a fixed mindset regarding emotion-management skills, the idea that "successful" people have figured out how to be happy all the time, and impatience. Let's investigate some of the types of self-criticism about emotions that might arise. Do any of these views sound familiar?

- "I shouldn't feel this way."
- "I'm not good at handling negative emotions."
- "Lots of people have much worse things to deal with, so I shouldn't feel bad about this."
- "Why can't I be more like so-and-so, who seems to have a way better attitude than I do, and to handle life so much better?"

- "Other people don't torture themselves like this."
- "I tried out a certain strategy one time for handling difficult feelings, and it didn't work, so that means that the strategy isn't any good or that I'm so miserably bad at this that no strategy can help me."
- "Why aren't I feeling better faster?"
- "I should really be handling this better."

These statements have a common element of self-criticism about your feelings and the way that you handle them. You might notice them as conscious thoughts, or they might reflect hidden assumptions. Practicing new ways of relating to emotional pain can help replace these beliefs with more effective habits and attitudes. And because the thoughts above include other subtle traps besides basic self-criticism, it's worth dismantling each misconception.

"I shouldn't feel this way." Let's unpack this one a bit because it can reflect a few different judgments. First, there's the idea that it's possible or easy to feel happy all of the time. The evidence does indeed show that with specific methods, people are capable of reducing difficult feelings and improving their well-being. But that doesn't mean that there will never be moments of emotional pain. For that reason, it's wise to cultivate some acceptance for difficult feelings.

By "acceptance" I don't mean commending painful emotions but rather allowing them to be there. You could think of it as shifting from "I shouldn't feel this way" to "This is the way that I feel right now, in this moment." You might check in with yourself about what feelings seem "acceptable" and which ones you "shouldn't" be having. Those assumptions reflect cultural conditioning: what feelings are okay to have as a man, as a woman, or as a "good" or "successful" person, parent, child, or spouse. You might only allow yourself to experience a narrow slice of feelings on the emotional spectrum. Perhaps you're convinced that if you let yourself feel something like anger or jealousy, it means something negative about you.

"I shouldn't feel this way" can also reflect a self-judgment that you're overreacting. That is, the intensity of emotion seems like an excessive response to what happened. Your partner left the dishes on the table, leaving you to clean up the mess, and you become irate. Most likely, you're not angry because this happened one time but because this time was one of many and because you're interpreting the behavior as meaning something.

An "overreaction" really means that someone is reacting both to the current situation and to other related problems and thoughts. Because we're not computers with the capacity to clear our browser histories, this is going to happen quite a bit. Instead of blaming yourself for "overreacting," you might just try noticing: "Huh. It seems like I'm having a feeling that feels tied to both this current situation and also to other experiences and thoughts." This strategy might also prevent judgment toward other people for "overreacting." What seems like an outsized reaction is more likely to be the combination of a reaction to the current situation plus a long, complex history of other feelings and experiences.

Finally, the judgment "I shouldn't feel this way" might be hiding other thoughts and feelings inside. "I shouldn't feel this way" might really mean "I'm scared to feel this way, because I don't know to handle it, and if I let myself feel bad, I might not be able to ever stop." But it will! One of the upsides of allowing yourself to notice and connect with more feelings is that you can notice the subtleties of how strong they are, what physical sensations are present, and how those change over time. For instance, one student reflected:

> I was in a trance of painfully constricting beliefs and emotions. Becoming aware of what emotions I feel— and where in my body I feel them—instigates a sense of hope that I can release my negative emotions. I have a habit of pushing my emotions away rather than feeling them because they can be painful and debilitating. However, practicing this emotional recognition actually allowed me to release major tension that had been building in my chest. Self-compassion began to naturally arise when I noticed my suffering.

"I'm not good at handling negative emotions." This self-criticism reflects a fixed mindset about emotion regulation: either you're good at handling negative emotions or you're not, and that's it. However, emotional regulation skills aren't a fixed trait, like eye color. They correspond to modeling (how you've observed other important people manage their emotions) and to practice (either repeating your current habits or trying out new skills on purpose).

There's also a strong sense of "I" in this statement. It's as though there's a default setting of "But what does this mean about me, about my character, about the kind of person I am, or about how good I am at this?" Can you try out the opposite idea? That is, what if the way that you handle difficult feelings doesn't actually mean anything deep about you, besides that it reflects your current conditioning and habits?

You might investigate the function of "I'm good at this; I'm bad at this" as a style of thinking. It might generate a sense of control ("I know who I am, what I'm good at, and what I'm bad at") and identity. Such categorical thinking might function to save you from all of the hassle of learning how to cope in a new way; but ultimately, it's a limiting mindset that doesn't recognize your true capacity for change.

"Other People Have It Worse, so I Shouldn't Feel Bad." Human suffering is not a contest. The fact that other people might be in the midst of losing a family member, their homes, their jobs, or even their lives doesn't erase what you're going through. Instead of helping you feel better, thinking that "other people have it worse" can invalidate your feelings or add guilt and self-criticism on top of the current hardship.

You might be criticizing yourself for fretting about minor details, like not having had a chance to return a phone call or for gaining a few pounds. "Minor details" might actually reflect important themes that are worthy of your attention. Maybe you're feeling disconnected in your friendships or struggling to take good care of your body in the context of other life demands. You might take a bit of time to sit with the feeling, and to explore if there is a larger issue underneath the more immediate "small" concern.

Dismissing "small" hardships also isn't a great habit for relating to other people. Would you want a friend to say to you, "Just remember, other people have it worse?" That doesn't seem very understanding or comforting. If you're noticing something, that means that it has affected you. Can you notice the feeling just as it is without either minimizing it or analyzing what it could mean about you?

"Why can't I be more like so-and-so, who handles things so much better?" During one of my jobs as a young adult, my cubicle faced my coworker's. She seemed happy all of the time, whereas I was often unhappy or in a mixed mood. I felt a huge gulf between her emotional mindset and mine. Ugh!

Why couldn't I just switch personalities with her? Hers was clearly just way better. Or maybe I could just *be* her, instead of having to slog through being me?

If you're in pain, it's normal to wish for a different experience. I don't know if my coworker was born with her cheerful disposition, or how her life experiences might have shaped her attitude. In any case, despite the many stories and movies where characters switch into another life, it seems unlikely that I could magically become another person. I have to work with the emotional vulnerabilities, habits, and opportunities that I've got.

You can be inspired by the way another person handles life without the same flavor of self-criticism of "Why can't I be more like that person?" There have been times when I've attended a meditation workshop with very experienced meditation teachers or talks by other leaders who seem calm and wise. Sometimes I sense a kind of peace, groundedness, or patience that leads me to feel more of those qualities myself, or at least to feel as though those qualities are possible. But the question "Why can't I be more like that other person?" conveys a judgment that however I am isn't okay, along with the unreasonable assumption that I can just choose another mindset and zap right to it, without doing the emotional work required to get there.

"Other people don't torture themselves like this." Oh, but they do. Not everyone, perhaps, but an enormous number of people struggle with self-criticism about how they're managing (or struggling to manage) their thoughts and feelings. You just don't see it.

This is a classic example of comparing your insides to other people's outsides. On the outside, other people seem less complicated. You might see others as "three-dimensional," but your own mind can feel more like fifty-seven dimensions. We're socialized not to share all of those parts with other people at once, and not to share some of them at all. And that simplification, necessary for most conversations and interactions, can leave us feeling alone in all of our complexity and inner conflicts.

Jobs like mine (being a therapist, and teaching university classes on mindfulness and compassion) offer windows into others' self-critical thinking and other mental turmoil. My patients and my students describe self-criticism and inner conflict so often that I view these as common mental states. But the slim portion of others' lives that are viewed on Facebook, Instagram, and even in person can make it seem as though everyone else's lives are more internally calm and coherent. It's a mirage. They're dealing with stuff, too.

"I tried out a new strategy, but it didn't work." Maybe trying a new strategy didn't work in the past. Maybe you didn't like it, or it didn't seem like a good fit. It might have been a difficult time to try a new strategy. When things are really hard, it can be too challenging to investigate a new way of coping. I recommend practicing new coping skills when you are experiencing mild to medium levels of emotional difficulty.

Perhaps the issue was that you only tried it only once or twice. In order to really benefit from a new way of handling things, it's usually necessary to practice the new strategy several times. But that requires some patience, as well as the ability to tolerate some level of discomfort before the new exercise becomes more comfortable.

"I should really be handling this better." This one came up for me recently, so I had a fresh opportunity to investigate it. I think that this idea contains some hidden assumptions, such as, "The fact that I'm not handling my emotions more skillfully means I'm bad." A self-critical mindset can use not

handling feelings "perfectly" as evidence that there's something wrong with me.

Finding myself somewhat trapped in the idea that I should be handling things better, I tried to ponder the question: "Is it truly the case that a person could handle this hardship more skillfully than I am handling it now?" The answer that arose was "Yes, but this is where you are now." I'm not the number-one best handler of emotional pain in the universe. I have plenty of growing and learning yet to do. So the question becomes, "Can I allow myself to be where I'm at, both with these emotions and how I'm managing them, while also gently recognizing true areas for growth?"

Perhaps there is a more skillful way to manage whatever emotion is arising. However, skills often take practice to develop, and harsh self-criticism rarely helps the process along. You might find yourself interpreting the challenge of managing difficult feelings along the lines of, "I'm bad at this, and that's awful!" A more constructive response might sound more like, "Yes, it's true that I, like many other people, can keep developing my skills in this area. For today, this is where I am."

Emotion Myths and Challenge Statements

Emotion myths are ideas about emotions—held either consciously or unconsciously—that shape how we relate to emotions.[4] Although these myths aren't true, they can feel true, and they can influence our behavior. Examples of emotion myths include the ideas that there is one correct emotional response for every situation, that seeking support is a sign of weakness, or that negative feelings are inherently wrong or overly dramatic. The writer Amy Clover observes that we tell ourselves stories about particular emotions: if we feel hurt, we're overly sensitive, thin-skinned, or unmanly; if we feel anger, we're crazy, out of control, or difficult; if we're disappointed, that means we're a pessimist; and if we feel fear, that means we're weak. Clover notes that she repeats to herself, "It's OK for me to feel this."[5]

To build healthier relationships with emotions, the psychologist Marsha Linehan encourages people to develop "challenge statements" that revise emotion myths.[6] For instance, if you hold the belief that there's one right way to feel in every circumstance, you could try out the challenge statement, "There are many normal ways to feel in the same situation." To challenge the belief that negative feelings are inherently wrong, you might develop the challenge statement, "A full range of feelings is a fundamental part of being human."

One of my students described implementing a challenge statement to the myth of needing to "tough it out" during times of stress:

An obstacle to self-compassion that I've found challenging is that I try to "tough it out" when I'm upset or dealing with a setback, which I think comes from a fear of weakness. Instead of being gentle to myself, I often think "just suck it up and get over it." This usually just makes me feel exhausted and irritable. I've been dealing with this by encouraging myself to cry when I feel like I need to instead of holding it in. I've also been trying to acknowledge my own feelings and tell myself that it's okay to be upset over a setback situation. Something I've found very self-comforting is standing in front of the mirror and saying, "I feel upset about _____, and that's okay because _____." I think working on being gentle and kind toward myself can help me shift away from the "suck it up" mindset going forward.

Building New Ways to Handle Feelings without Self-Criticism

How can you try allowing all feelings, skillfully? Make space—in your mind, your body, and your schedule—to first notice feelings, and then to be kind toward yourself as you experience those feelings. It doesn't have to be only about allowing feelings that are deeply upsetting or the ones that you feel shouldn't be there. The idea of allowing all feelings means that you're also open to subtler feelings, and even open to pleasant or neutral feelings as well. It's easy to think that you only feel whatever sensation feels most intense, and to disregard other feelings.

As you open to the feelings that you're experiencing in this moment, you might notice that some sensations feel relatively pleasant, some feel unpleasant to different degrees, and some feel neutral. That is, you can notice a feeling that doesn't seem particularly pleasant or unpleasant; it's just there. By encouraging people to experience their feelings, I'm not advocating that they prioritize emotional pain. Noticing what feels neutral or positive, even during stressful times, can be balancing. It might just take a bit of practice. It might seem unimportant: Why would I take the time or mental energy to notice how my foot feels in my sock or how the air feels on my skin?

Allowing all feelings skillfully refers to noticing how you're feeling in this moment. So, by "all feelings," I'm not suggesting that you open up all at once to a lifetime of feelings, where you reexperience every hardship from the past and everything that could go wrong in the future. That's way too much to handle. The idea is to try to feel what bodily sensations and emotions are present just right here, right now, in this very moment. I don't think it's possible to have awareness for every aspect of experience, but you can try allowing and noticing what you can.

After you notice the feelings right now, in this very moment, you can go ahead and notice your feelings in the next moment, and then in the one after that. Try to do that without any expectation that they either change or stay the same. If you do this for several moments in a row, you're bound to notice some changes, because bodily sensations and emotions rarely stay exactly the same. Allowing all feelings means being open to feeling different in this moment than you were in the last one, or in the next one. Observing those changes, even if they're subtle, can confer a sense of hope, a lived contrast to the sense that feelings of depression, anxiety, or anger will last forever, unchanging.

The practices that I describe below offer structured ways to experience your feelings in the present moment. The self-compassion break, created by psychologist Kristin Neff, involves acknowledging suffering, remembering that emotional pain is a normal part of being human, and responding to your feelings with self-kindness. The RAIN practice, as developed by mindfulness teacher Michele McDonald and described by the psychologist and mindfulness teacher Tara Brach, outlines a sequence of steps for recognizing feelings, allowing them to be present, investigating them with a caring and interested attitude, and nurturing feelings with self-compassion. Finally, seated breath meditation, introduced in chapter 3, can be used to practice allowing all feelings without judging them.

Self-Compassion Break

This exercise is short. You take a moment to identify with some aspect of life that doesn't feel great right now. Your mind might jump readily to the hardest situation or worry in your life right now. But if this is your first time with this exercise, it can help to pick something that's a bit more moderate rather than going straight for the heaviest (emotional) weights at the gym.

You can bring the issue or situation to your mind and also to your body. Take a minute to just notice the feelings right now, in this moment. What does it feel like inside your mind and inside your body? Can you just notice those sensations for a minute, without getting swept up in any complex thinking?

You can acknowledge that the feeling or situation is difficult or that you are suffering. It can help to have an actual phrase. Kristin Neff suggests, "This is a moment of suffering" or "This is hard."[7] You might feel relief in admitting that pain is present.

The next step in the self-compassion break involves acknowledging that "suffering is a part of life." That is, it's a regular part of being human, rather than an experience that separates you from other people or marks you as defective. Suffering is a part of life, and you're alive, so you will suffer sometimes. From a Buddhist perspective, this acknowledgment reflects the First Noble Truth: that part of life includes *dukkha*, often translated as "suffering," "difficulty," "unhappiness," "pain," "anxiety," "unsatisfactoriness," "struggle," or "stressfulness." Several mindfulness teachers have observed that it seems especially common in Western cultures for that dissatisfaction to be expressed as self-criticism or self-loathing—the sense that "there's something wrong with me."[8]

Finally, the last step is to offer yourself some kindness about your feelings. The idea of offering kindness might seem abstract, especially if you're not used to it. Using words can help make the practice more concrete. You could silently say to yourself, "Oh, I'm sorry you're going through this hard time," or "I care about how you're feeling in this moment," or "I'm here, and I want to help."

Self-compassion reflects an ability to acknowledge and remain present with whatever is happening inside, even if the feelings are very painful, and to treat ourselves with care and love in stressful moments. It takes some practice, but that practice can pay off: self-compassion is strongly related to well-being, motivation, and accomplishments, and is linked with fewer mental health problems. In fact, the research evidence shows that the impact of self-compassion on mental health is about ten times greater than the impact of mindfulness.[9] Just a few weeks of practice can meaningfully increase people's self-compassion and reduce their stress. For instance, research investigating a seven-day self-compassion intervention for athletes demonstrated decreases in their self-criticism, concern about mistakes, and rumination.[10]

With practice, the self-compassion break can become integrated into everyday stressful experiences, so that when stress happens, it feels less alienating and overwhelming. Proactively deciding upon strategies for moments of hardship, practicing those strategies, and then implementing them is empowering. It doesn't make suffering disappear, but it's a world away from having no strategies at all, or ineffective ones. Over time, self-compassion becomes a reflex—a resilient muscle that helps us stay strong during moments of stress.

You can imagine yourself driving after a long and particularly stressful day, when someone suddenly cuts right in front of you. Your heartbeat rapidly accelerates; you try to regain your equilibrium; and you become angry (perhaps uttering a few choice words). Without a sense of self-compassion or practiced strategies, you might stay in that state of increased stress and anger. Alternatively, you could take a moment to pause and reflect that "yup, that was really scary. I was understandably afraid of crashing the car just then. Plus, I'm already feeling stressed, tired, and hungry right now. It makes sense that I feel this way, and my feelings are a normal part of being human. Now, I can try being especially caring toward myself in this moment. I can find some kindness or sympathy for my own feelings. And perhaps ask myself, 'What do I need? Water? When I get home, would it feel nourishing to take a few minutes to calm down, and then perhaps to connect with a friend on the phone?'"

Core Exercise

SELF-COMPASSION BREAK[11]

To practice the self-compassion break, call a stressful circumstance to mind. When you first start to practice this exercise, pick a situation that involves a medium amount of stress rather than the one that's the most stressful for you. Then:

1. Acknowledge that you are suffering.
2. Remember that suffering is part of being human—a shared experience, even though our own particular suffering often feels alienating.
3. Offer some form of kindness to yourself about your feelings, either in the form of words ("I'm so sorry you have to go through this"), an action that could help (such as a cup of tea or a walk) or soothing touch (like massaging your neck or putting your hand on your heart).

RAIN

This exercise, originally developed by mindfulness teacher Michele McDonald, uses the acronym RAIN to structure it into four steps: recognizing feelings, allowing them, showing interest, and maintaining non-identification with emotions. Another meditation teacher, Tara Brach, has the acronym stand for recognize, allow, investigate, nurture. Either version of RAIN can provide a helpful structure for observing and relating to feelings. I've attempted to integrate both versions into the descriptions of the RAIN approach below.

The first step is to *recognize* what is going on. Sometimes it's obvious what feelings are present, but some feelings are more subtle. When you pause to recognize what's happening, you try to gently note the physical sensations, emotions, thoughts, and behaviors that are affecting you right in this moment. You can observe what arises most strongly into your awareness.

Next, you *allow* your experiences to be there, exactly as they are. This has to do with your attitude toward your feelings. The idea is to allow them, to make room, and to let them exist. Instead of fixing or changing them, or even telling yourself to "let them go," you let the experiences be present. Tara Brach offers that during this step, you might say to yourself, "It's okay" or "This belongs." This step prepares you to deepen your attention toward your feelings.

The third step is to *investigate* your feelings with *interest* and care. This means bringing a sense of curiosity and care to the experience, asking yourself: "What do I notice most? Where do I feel this in my body? What thoughts or beliefs emerge?" However, try not to get too wrapped up in mental analysis or the backstory of why you feel the way that you do. Instead, try to stay with your present-moment embodied sensations, of "what do these feelings themselves feel like, right in this moment?"

As a last step, you can try either *non-identifying* (remembering that thoughts and feelings are passing events rather than who we are) or *nurturing* with self-compassion. Brach explains that this might look like forgiveness, or just being present in companionship, or comfort. If you find it daunting to be a source of love toward yourself, you might think of someone else who has been kind, understanding, or comforting toward you in your life and imagining that care cascading into you.

Core Exercise

RAIN

1. <u>R</u>ecognize what feelings and sensations are present in this moment.
2. <u>A</u>llow the experience to be what it is in this moment, just as it is.
3. <u>I</u>nvestigate or show <u>I</u>nterest in your feelings, in a caring and nonjudgmental way.
4. <u>N</u>urture your feelings with care and compassion, and maintain Non-Identification (that is, refrain from viewing your feelings as though they are who you are rather than passing events.

I teach both the self-compassion break and the RAIN technique in my mindfulness and compassion courses, and it's interesting to hear how these practices come alive in my students' experiences. One student shared this account:

The RAIN meditation allowed me to really try to become aware and in tune with my own emotion. Its first step, which is to Recognize what's going on, allows me to really sit with myself and think, "Okay, what is this feeling that I'm feeling?" The second step is my favorite, actually, because it is to Allow the experience to be there, just as it is. I like this step and find this step particularly helpful for me, because I tend to struggle with letting myself experience emotions. I think that I, and a lot of us, recognize that we are experiencing a negative or unpleasant emotion and immediately try to put it down, suppress it, or medicate it. This practice showed me the importance of actually letting myself feel emotions so that I am able to get to the root of the problem, as opposed to cosmetically "fixing" it.

Breathing Meditation for Allowing All Feelings

As described in chapter 3, meditation offers another way of allowing all feelings—while simultaneously building emotion regulation skills and reducing self-criticism. A common meditation method is to focus on the present-moment sensations of breathing while nonjudgmentally observing any other thoughts and feelings that arise, and then refocusing back on the breath. The act of allowing the full experience of physical sensations, such as breathing, seems to help people fully allow thoughts and feelings as well.

Allowing all feelings is an important facet of breathing meditation. The idea is to find a "middle way" in which you neither push away experiences nor hold on to them. Although some forms of breathing meditation involve trying to breathe in a specific way, a common instruction is to simply notice the breath and its qualities (long, short, shallow, deep, or else sensations in the chest, nose, etc.). The practice of allowing a full range of breathing sensations, without trying to control them, can pave the way to allowing a full range of emotional sensations to be present as well, rather than constricting emotions with inner editing or self-criticism.

The mindfulness teacher Larry Rosenberg describes engaging a particular intention while using breathing meditation to allow all feelings skillfully:

> The ultimate goal—though this is no easy thing and takes time to develop—is to allow everything to come up, with all its energy: all of, for instance, your anger and loneliness and despair, to allow these things to arise and be transformed by the light of awareness.
>
> There is tremendous energy in these states, and much of the time we suppress them, so that we not only lose all the energy that is in them but also expend a great deal keeping them down. What we gradually learn is to let these things come up and be transformed, to release their energy. You don't solve your problems in this practice, it is sometimes said, you dissolve them. But the wild mind that we all confront when we start discourages many practitioners.[12]

Cultivating the skill of noticing each breath, without judging it, can generalize to noticing other feelings without judging them. It's a subtle form of exposure therapy, because it gradually interrupts a style of distancing yourself from feelings. It's less scary to "go there," because you've already been there. You get used to your own tendencies to gravitate toward certain kinds of thoughts and feelings, and more confident that you can notice those tendencies gently, without panicking about them. The available evidence underscores that breathing meditation can decrease reactivity to difficult thoughts and feelings.[13]

Military veterans with post-traumatic stress report having a different relationship with their emotions after practicing breathing meditation and other mindfulness techniques. One study gathered veterans' reflections after six weeks of practice. Participants' observations included:

> "Symptoms have not changed but my response to them has changed. Most notable change is the process of dealing with them."
> "I am able to step back, calm down, not enrage as would have been the case before."
> "[I] don't get angry as often and it is easier to cool down."[14]

You can gently discern which practice seems like a good place to explore at this point in your life. Even though the self-compassion break and RAIN practices are specifically designed to help people notice, allow, and be kinder and less judgmental toward their feelings, people often report similar results from mediation that uses the breath as its focus. In fact, it could even feel less emotionally charged to work on allowing feelings to arise with breathing meditation rather than through the self-compassion break or RAIN, because the breath can seem like a more neutral topic than your own difficult feelings.

Allowing Secondary Emotions, Skillfully and Sometimes

Often, one emotion leads to another; we have a feeling about a feeling. These are sometimes called secondary emotions or meta-emotions. The complex, multilayered experience of emotions can be overwhelming. It can be hard to notice one type of emotional sensation in the tangle of interconnected thoughts and interpretations clamoring for attention. Buddhist psychology includes the idea of a mental "second arrow" that worsens the original wound. The mindfulness teacher Thich Nhat Hanh explains that "the second arrow, fired by our own selves, is our reaction, our storyline, and our anxiety. All these things magnify the suffering."[15]

Patients who come to therapy with anxiety often have a mix of feelings that can be viewed through the lens of primary and secondary emotions. Patients often describe "primary" anxiety feelings as unpleasant physical sensations (such as a racing heart, sweating, or feeling shaky) that can arise during moments of anxiety or panic. But perhaps even more painful are the feelings of disconnection ("I'm not normal"), anxiety about the anxiety (such as fear that it will never improve), and a mix of other emotional reactions toward anxiety (including despair, anger, rejection, and frustration). The evidence indicates that negative secondary emotions, or painful emotions about your emotions, are linked with lower levels of well-being.[16]

Sometimes secondary emotions are inevitable, but not always. Even though it's very challenging, building the habit of kindly allowing anxiety can prevent some of the other emotional responses from arising, because those responses are linked with viewing the anxiety as unacceptable. Practicing allowing anxiety kindly can begin to quell secondary emotions about it. Instead of experiencing a combination of unpleasant physical sensations, disconnection, anxiety about the anxiety, despair, self-judgment, and frustration, the anxiety experience by itself becomes easier. Handling the physical symptoms alone—in a kind way—is much easier than managing the whole array of suffering.

There are times when it can be helpful to allow and notice secondary emotions. If you become so frustrated or angry that you snap at someone you care about, you might find you then feel guilty, embarrassed, sad, disappointed with yourself, and concerned that you've upset your loved one. None of those feelings are fun to experience. But they might be useful. They could help signal you that you need to apologize to the person to whom you spoke harshly, and they might help motivate you to handle your frustration differently next time.

Secondary emotions might arise as a defensive function to protect you against other emotions.[17] You might feel angry toward a friend who hasn't called, in part to protect yourself from feeling hurt. Or perhaps you feel enraged or disgusted by voters who don't agree with you, in part because you fear what could happen if their preferred laws or politicians were to win. Practices like RAIN that involve investigating present-moment sensations often uncover primary emotions underneath secondary ones.

You can also consciously cultivate helpful secondary emotions. Practices that help cultivate compassion, including the self-compassion break and the RAIN technique, are actually about intentionally building secondary emotions. Instead of falling into habitual secondary emotions, such as worrying about your painful feelings, you're purposefully nourishing a tendency to respond with particular secondary emotions, such as kindness and understanding toward your own suffering.

Allowing Yourself to Feel Bad

It can be scary to allow yourself to feel unhappy. You might be concerned that it will never stop. You might expect that one bad feeling will simply lead to another, and to another. But you may find that allowing feelings is actually less painful than not allowing them. The meditation teacher David Young observes that many people "skim" their feelings, like a hand skimming over water, but they find that the constant irritation of surface contact can feel like torture. He notes that fewer people dive in and feel their emotions more fully. Young elaborates:

> Resisting the urge to skim our feelings and instead dive deep way down can allow those feelings to go away or reduce much quicker than we'd realize. Kind of like how much more painful it is wading into a freezing cold pool versus plunging in. Additionally, when we take these deep dives they become progressively easier and less painful while leaving us with greater wisdom and a sense of wholeness. We "feel" more of ourselves nonjudgmentally and we can therefore more fully "be" ourselves.[18]

The mindfulness teacher La Sarmiento explains how diving deep into their pain after heartbreak paved the way toward self-acceptance.[19] La, who identifies as genderqueer, observed that at age six, "I didn't want to be a little girl," and remembered having the sense that "there was something not quite right." La recalled that the message that they told themselves was, "If anyone knew who you really were, no one would ever love you or accept you," and that they carried that belief into their relationships as an adult, settling for "whoever would love me." After several failed relationships, La decided to take some time "to really allow myself to feel that loneliness, that sense of being unlovable or unacceptable."

La explains that it was necessary to "fully embrace that suffering" in order to figure out what was going on and how to take care of themselves. La notes that the mindfulness teacher Ajahn Chah said that "when you sit, let it be what you are . . . if you haven't wept deeply, you haven't begun to meditate." By allowing themselves to fully acknowledge and experience feelings of immense pain, alienation, fear, and self-rejection, La was able to cultivate a more authentic relationship with themselves: "To really be aware of what's happening, and to express feelings and needs." As a result of having committed to staying open and present with some of their most painful feelings, La was able to enter a long-term relationship in which they are "the most myself that I've ever been with anyone—fully myself."

Can Allowing Difficult Feelings Really Help You Feel Better?

It might seem hard to believe, but there's a great deal of research evidence that allowing and accepting difficult feelings is positively associated with well-being. In one study that included over a thousand adults, the habit of accepting mental experiences was linked to higher levels of mental health and life satisfaction, even after controlling for related variables such as rumination and reappraisal.[20] Other studies demonstrate accepting thoughts and feelings leads to lower negative emotional responses to both laboratory and daily stress, even after accounting for factors such as the amount of life stress, socioeconomic status, gender, and ethnicity.[21]

Why does letting yourself experience difficult thoughts and feelings lead to better mental health and well-being? Researchers Daniel Evans and Suzanne Segerstrom investigated the question "Why do mindful people worry less?" They reported that refraining from judgmental thoughts decreases the elaborations and interpretations that elicit additional thoughts.[22] Scientists describe a similar process in the realm of emotions. Acceptance reduces tendencies to react to your own feelings with agitation, self-criticism, anxiety, or despair—responses that can worsen or prolong negative emotions. Refraining from reacting strongly toward your own thoughts and emotions seems to lessen their intensity, so that thoughts and emotions subside more quickly.[23]

Sometimes letting yourself feel bad doesn't seem like it's necessary, especially if the situation only involves seemingly minor amounts of pain. Today, I was feeling upset for reasons that didn't feel worthy enough to "really" feel bad. With only a few quiet moments available, I decided to meditate. I had a skeptical attitude going in. ("Since I only have a few minutes to meditate, it probably won't do much.") But in the spirit of this chapter, I asked myself, "How about *letting* yourself feel bad and really allowing whatever hard feelings exist to be really and truly bad, if they're in there?" I had a few wavelike sensations in my chest, and then I cried. For about five seconds. Really, not even ten. And then I felt way better: my chest seemed less tight, and things felt less impossible. I know that crying isn't something everyone does, but there are times that it can help. But to get there, I had to choose to allow myself to feel bad. And then I felt quite a bit better.

During one of my recent classes, a student described how she worked on allowing herself to feel bad following the end of a relationship. A key aspect involved letting herself be in the middle of her grief process rather than pressuring herself to have resolved her feelings:

> I had been so hard on myself to put in the post-relationship breakup work of processing all that had happened in the relationship and I was pressuring myself to be in the "healed" place. This journal session allowed me to take a necessary pause and feel how consuming (of energy and time) self-criticism can be. I was also able to see how easy being kind to myself was and how it was something that took less energy. I found that the whole time I was trying to "heal" my focus was on being in the "healed place" rather than the journey of healing itself.

Allowing "bad" feelings can have the unintended effect of allowing more positive ones in as well. Mindfulness practice seems to reduce the mind's emphasis on negative thoughts.[24] I recently had the opportunity to practice allowing difficult feelings when after his first twenty months at home, my youngest child started day care this week. He was clearly apprehensive, confused, and upset during drop-off, and I worried that he would feel sad and even abandoned. Once I got home, I couldn't focus on my work. I cleaned. I walked. I practiced lovingkindness meditation for him, as a way of transforming my rumination into well-wishing. And I also knew that I had to allow myself to feel bad, to sit with the uncertainty of his adjustment, with my awareness of his suffering, and with my own suffering.

I sat down with the intention to let myself really feel the agony of it all, to fully allow the pain, within the safe space of accepting my emotions just as they were, focusing on present-moment feelings and sensations, witnessing my feelings with an awareness larger than the emotions themselves, and maintaining an attitude of self-kindness. I checked in with the question, "What's happening right now in my body?" I noticed feelings in the left part of my chest, as though there were gears over my heart that were stuck. I breathed. I observed some constriction in my throat. I breathed. It wasn't fun, but these sensations felt manageable rather than devastating. Then my stomach made some weird gurgling noises. And then what came up were some feelings of gladness, of lightness in my chest, and thoughts about how much I like my son's new teacher, who said that she would show my son pictures of her pet rabbit, Gordo, if he seemed upset. I felt respect and gratitude toward all of the staff members at the day care, and happiness for my son to connect with them. Even though I had begun my practice with the intention to really let myself feel the "bad stuff," the "good stuff" arose as well.

———

The self-compassion break, the RAIN technique, and breathing meditation each offer a skillful way to open up to difficult feelings. Allowing all feelings (skillfully) is a radical alternative to suppressing them, minimizing them, distracting yourself, ruminating, worrying about your feelings, or criticizing yourself for having challenging feelings. Practicing a strategy many times can promote a sense of confidence, so that you can get from "I'm not good at handling difficult emotions," to "I have a method that I've used before and that I can use to get through a rough patch." The strategies themselves also cultivate kindness toward yourself and reduce self-criticism. Whether you use challenge statements for emotion myths, the self-compassion break, the RAIN technique, or breathing meditation, your mental efforts can transform both your attitude toward your feelings and even the feelings themselves.

Sometimes the practice of "allowing all feelings" might seem like a hodgepodge. I recently had a quiet twenty minutes when I was in a relatively neutral state of mind, and I sat down with the intention of allowing all feelings to be present. I noticed feelings in my face: tension around my eyelids, tightness in the way that I was holding my jaw, and a bit of itchiness in my scalp. Going deeper into the eyelid tension, I felt the grip of the veins and skin over my eyes, the heat, the charge, the tightness. I felt a little bit of a headache, but also some appreciation that it had improved over the more intense headache of a couple of hours before. I wondered and worried for a few seconds about the schedule for the coming week. I heard a bird chirping and noticed that I enjoyed the sound of it. Other thoughts arose: gladness for my kids to be out at the beach at this very moment . . . and then concern for family members evacuating from wildfires. Then fear, frustration, and hopelessness about environmental crises, showing up like a drag on my heart and an ache in my bones. Tension in my toes. A deeper breath. A sensation of breathing that feels a bit heavy. Other parts of my body— legs, back, feeling healthy and strong even as my breathing feels heavy. A recognition that my concerns and feelings are normal. Kindness and warmth toward myself about how I'm feeling in this moment. Feeling daunted and unsure about how to communicate with kids about climate change in a truthful yet hopeful manner—the fear that I'll do it wrong, an urge to plan what to say. Back to this moment, appreciating the space of silence, appreciating my breathing. Noticing feelings in this moment, and the next, and the next. Using my breath as an anchor to keep returning to my feelings in this moment instead of future plans and concerns, over and over again.

After sitting for that session, I felt connected to my bodily sensations and more synched up to my moment-to-moment experience. I did not solve climate change, or eliminate my fear and frustration about it, or figure out how to talk to my kids about it. But my stress seemed less whirlwindy. I had a sensation of openness in my chest, and as though there was plenty of room in that moment to feel my feelings. I also felt a sort of cushion of kindness around my feelings, just as they were.

Living in the Zone of Allowing All Feelings, Skillfully

Adam was a graduate student at my university, but he was a bit further along in his studies than I was, and he had an easygoing and cheerful presence that I admired. He also seemed able to face the reality of pain in a brave way—both when it emerged for patients in our clinic and among our fellow graduate students. Adam seemed at ease with himself and at ease with others. I found him easy to talk to. He was one of those people who just seem to "get it" without needing too many explanations.

One of the perks of being in the psychology field is getting to know many different colleagues who are great listeners and who like to explore complex emotions, and I'd occasionally chat with Adam about my own romantic hopes and disappointments. I was surprised when Adam told me he had just broken up with his partner of six years, a girlfriend with whom he had lived and planned to spend the rest of his life. But I was even more surprised with his response when I asked him how he was doing. He said, "I feel awful. Every day is hard. But I also know it's my job to be really, really sad right now."

"It's my job to be really, really sad right now." I'd never heard anything like that before. Not just that it's okay to be sad, but that it is actually *necessary* work to be with challenging feelings and not just to run from them or to change them into something positive immediately. It seemed to reflect a certain truth and maturity that seem to be in short supply after most relationships. People often feel pressure to prove both to themselves and to others that they're "over" their exes. This seemed different. Plus, from his words, he knew that the pain wouldn't last forever. It was the genuine truth of the "right now," but it wasn't a life sentence.

Adam indicated that he was in pain, but he wasn't rushing himself to have more positive feelings. His acceptance of just where he was emotionally seemed to fit with the way that he showed up for his patients. For instance, in our clinical practice group of graduate-student therapists, he had talked about providing counseling for siblings whose mom was dying, and having an attitude of "Yes, this is deeply and immensely horrible. It sucks and it hurts and it's overwhelming, and I'll sit right here with you as we face this together." There was power simply in his company, in his steadfast not running away from awful feelings or painting over them—either for others or for himself. You might think that allowing pain to be there could make the pain take over, but instead, his patience seemed to make it more bearable. It wasn't all tangled up with censorship, denial, and self-judgment. It was free to be there and to taper off with time and new experiences.

Adam graduated a few years later. His new partner, now his wife, was in the audience, and he held their baby girl in his arms as he accepted his diploma. I recently saw him at a conference, looking grayer and happier than ever.

REFLECTION QUESTIONS

1. Have you ever told yourself to "get over it"? Did that work?
2. Are there certain emotions that you allow yourself to experience and other ones that you don't? Which ones do you put in each category?
3. Was there a time or situation when you gave yourself permission to have and to feel the full range of your emotions? What was that like?
4. Do you notice times when you restrict your emotions by numbing or distracting yourself?
5. Are there times when you feel lost in thoughts about your feelings, in which you fixate on repetitive material or feel deeply identified with your emotional state—as though you *are* your feelings?
6. What are some of your emotion myths (for instance, the idea that other people have it worse so you shouldn't complain, or that negative emotions are inherently bad or destructive)? Can you come up with phrases that challenge those myths, such as telling yourself that just because other people may face worse hardships doesn't mean that your feelings aren't real or acceptable, or that it's deeply human to feel a full range of emotion?

7. Can you tolerate painful feelings when your friends or family express them, without jumping to try to fix or solve them? Do you feel frustrated at how long it takes them to feel better, or if they seem to get stuck?
8. What is your initial response to self-compassion? Does the idea seem self-centered or cheesy? How does your initial response differ from your observations after you practice a self-compassion break?

7

Continuing Healthy Self-Talk

MOVING AWAY FROM constant self-criticism and toward kind, friendly, and encouraging self-talk is a big deal. After having lived for many years in the agony of evaluating myself unfavorably, even hating myself—all day long—it still amazes me to now have a mind that observes my mistakes and shortcomings graciously, and that encourages me to improve them without dwelling on them. And I continue to be delighted when hearing my students and patients describe similar arcs in their own self-talk journeys.

There are many ways to improve self-criticism besides the ones that I describe in this book. I encourage you to explore other avenues or to modify the ones that I've suggested. Working with a therapist is helpful for many people, in part because spending time with someone who treats you with encouragement, kindness, and acceptance can lead you to treat yourself in a similar manner. You might also try to "go in through the body," by incorporating other mind-body approaches (such as yoga, body scans, martial arts, or somatic therapy) that can help release bodily tension related to self-criticism. Many people also find that religious or spiritual practice assuages self-criticism. Prayer and related practices can interrupt default mental habits, and they can cultivate thought patterns that more closely reflect your deepest values. An emphasis on serving others, through volunteering or within your own work and relationships, can also reduce self-criticism and nurture happiness.

You don't need to practice healthy self-talk alone. Some of the exercises in this book are often practiced in community. For instance, many meditation centers offer group practice sessions to help cultivate nonjudgment and compassion, with both virtual and in-person options. There are also a number of eight-week classes that include practices to reduce self-criticism, both online and in person, including Mindful Self-Compassion, Compassion Cultivation Training, and Mindfulness-Based Stress Reduction. In many online and in-person events, people share their own stories of failing forward (for instance, the organization "fuckupnights.com" hosts events where speakers describe learning from failures in the workplace). You could also decide to practice spot the success or behavioral activation with a friend to help keep you on track, and to help you feel less alone in the quest to develop healthier self-talk.

Even after your mind shifts from predominantly self-critical to predominantly self-encouraging, you may have moments or periods where you find yourself being quite self-critical again. Those self-critical moments don't mean that all of your efforts were in vain. Practicing exercises such as the ones in this book can help reduce the frequency and severity of self-criticism, but they are unlikely to make it disappear entirely. If I inadvertently say something insensitive to a friend, I might note a pull toward imagining, "Oh no, they're going to hate me forever!" The deep draw toward self-criticism can be almost comforting in its familiarity, because it has been a strong part of my experience from an early age. Stress, hunger, or fatigue might increase the likelihood of falling back into old patterns. But with extensive awareness about self-criticism and experience with alternative self-talk practices, I'm more likely to notice that pull quickly and then to step back—to repair mistakes when I can, without jumping to self-critical or catastrophic conclusions.

Healthy self-talk supports new beginnings: mental energy that might otherwise be subsumed by self-criticism gets freed up for relationships, activities, and interests. I hope that you also spend time finding humor and joy. As passionate as I am about improving self-talk and addressing other aspects of mental health, it's also important to balance those efforts with moments in which you don't try to change anything about yourself but just experience being alive exactly as you are in the moment. I'm also cognizant that there is plenty in the world that urgently needs fixing, far beyond ourselves and our self-talk, and that it's necessary to figure out how to help.

The extent of suffering in the world can feel overwhelming, and it is understandable to either avoid it or to despair, even without a layer of self-criticism. Sometimes I practice sitting with the idea that there is no "good enough" action that I can take today to solve climate change, poverty, and racism—the reality is that whatever I do will truly not be good enough to make those problems disappear. The world's troubles aren't about me and whether I am good enough. I can allow myself to feel sadness, anger, and frustration about the many difficulties that exist while remembering that getting tangled up in self-evaluation can prevent helpful actions.

Specific, concrete actions, such as voting, contacting elected officials, or donating time or money, rather than focusing on reading a great deal of news, might feel energizing or hopeful, and external actions are more likely to make an impact than internal processes.

I wrote most this book during the coronavirus pandemic. It was interesting to observe my own and others' self-talk within this context. What does it mean to be doing "well" or treating myself kindly while coping with a pandemic? The stress of my own situation did not approach that of so many who lost loved ones or jobs, and yet it was sill stressful to try to homeschool my elementary-school child and my preschool kid, to see patients remotely while the baby napped, to teach online, to squeeze in ten or twenty minutes of writing at a time, and to worry about health, politics, and the situation throughout the world. The writing experience was certainly the opposite of the hours of quiet time to reflect and write peacefully that I had imagined.

I did sometimes feel self-critical of myself during the writing process, even as I consciously understood that I was doing my best amid a wild experience. Sometimes things will just be hard, and it won't be clear how to handle them. In the spring and summer of 2020, I took comfort from the Disney character Anna in the movie *Frozen II*, voiced by Kristen Bell, who sings to herself during moments of stress: "Just do the next right thing." As I wrote each chapter, I renewed my own practices with the skills that I was describing. Each time, I felt grateful to have a specific go-to technique, an anchor to boost my confidence and to decrease my stress and vulnerability to self-criticism.

Practice often fluctuates. Throughout the book I've emphasized repetition because the habit of self-criticism is so strong that changing it takes considerable practice. It's unusual to improve self-talk through intention or insight alone. Once self-criticism becomes less prominent, you might decide not to keep up the practices that you found helpful. It's also normal to practice a bit, to pause for a bit, and then to return to the same practice that you found helpful, or to try a variation or a new approach. I've really enjoyed the experience of getting back into practices that I know well but sometimes haven't tried in a week or a month, such as spot the success, the self-compassion break, or in-depth metta practice. There have been times in my life where I've practiced sitting meditation for thirty minutes or longer consistently, and other times when my formal practice was limited to a few rounds of "Inhale, my friend; exhale, my friend" per day. In whatever manner your self-talk unfolds, I hope that you can be gentle and encouraging toward yourself—rather than self-critical—about the amount, quality, consistency, and progression of your self-talk practice.

I wish you well, both with your self-talk and otherwise.

NOTES

Introduction

1. For this research, I used "The Forms of Self-Criticising/Attacking and Self-Reassuring Scale." (FSCRS); along with the PROMIS scales to measure depression and anxiety. See P. Gilbert, M. Clark, S. Hempel, J. N. V. Miles, and C. Irons, "Criticising and Reassuring Oneself: An Exploration of Forms, Styles and Reasons in Female Students, *British Journal of Clinical Psychology* 43 (2004): 31–50.

2. This research was reviewed by the Institutional Review Board at Seattle University.

3. This research was reviewed by the Institutional Review Board at Seattle University.

4. R. Trompetter, E. de Kleine, and E. T. Bohlmeijer, "Why Does Positive Mental Health Buffer Against Psychopathology? An Exploratory Study on Self-Compassion as a Resilience Mechanism and Adaptive Emotion Regulation Strategy," *Cognitive Therapy and Research* 41, no. 33 (2017): 459–68.

5. Y. Kotera, J. Dosedlova, D. Andrzejewski, G. Kaluzeviciute, and M. Sakai, "From Stress to Psychopathology: Relationship with Self-Reassurance and Self-Criticism in Czech University Students," *International Journal of Mental Health and Addiction* (2021): 1–12.

6. A. Zeeck, J. von Wietersheim, H. Weiss, S. Hermann, K. Endorf, I. Lau, and A. Hartmann, "Self-Criticism and Personality

Functioning Predict Patterns of Symptom Change in Major Depressive Disorder," *Frontiers in Psychiatry* 11 (March 2020): 147.

7. N. A. Rector, R. M. Bagby, Z. V. Segal, R. T. Joffe, and A. Levitt, "Self-Criticism and Dependency in Depressed Patients Treated with Cognitive Therapy or Pharmacotherapy," *Cognitive Therapy and Research* 24, no. 5 (2000): 571–84.

8. P. A. Resick, C. M. Monson, and K. M. Chard, *Cognitive Processing Therapy for PTSD: A Comprehensive Manual* (New York: Guilford Press, 2017), 6.

9. K. D. Neff and C. K. Germer, "A Pilot Study and Randomized Controlled Trial of the Mindful Self-Compassion Program," *Journal of Clinical Psychology* 69, no. 1 (2013): 28–44.

10. For example, see L. A. Weingartner, S. Sawning, M. A. Shaw, and J. B. Klein, "Compassion Cultivation Training Promotes Medical Student Wellness and Enhanced Clinical Care," *BMC Medical Education* 19, no. 1 (2019): 139

11. P. Gilbert, "The Origins and Nature of Compassion Focused Therapy," *British Journal of Clinical Psychology* 53, no. 1 (2014): 6–41.

12. K. E. Wakelin, G. Perman, and L. M. Simonds, "Effectiveness of Self-Compassion-Related Interventions for Reducing Self-Criticism: A Systematic Review and Meta-Analysis," *Clinical Psychology and Psychotherapy* 10 (March 2021).

13. "AWS Well-Architected Framework," Amazon, 2020, https://docs.aws.amazon.com/wellarchitected/latest/framework/welcome.html, accessed October 11, 2021.

14. K. D. Neff and R. Vonk, "Self-Compassion versus Global Self-Esteem: Two Different Ways of Relating to Oneself," *Journal of Personality* 77, no. 1 (2009): 23–50.

15. Neff and Vonk, "Self-Compassion versus Global Self-Esteem," 23–50.

16. "Larry Yang on Insight Meditation and Multiculturalism," July 31, 2013, YouTube video, 19:49, www.youtube.com/watch?v=F9JGWFKZOik&ab_channel=GarrisonInstitute.

17. Rick Hanson, *Hardwiring Happiness: The New Brain Science of Contentment, Calm, and Confidence* (New York: Harmony, 2016).

18. H. Du and E. Jonas, "Being Modest Makes You Feel Bad: Effects of the Modesty Norm and Mortality Salience on Self-Esteem in a Collectivistic Culture," *Scandinavian Journal of Psychology* 56, no. 1 (2014): 86–98.

19. See S. Kitayama and Y. Uchida, "Explicit Self-Criticism and Implicit Self-Regard: Evaluating Self and Friend in Two Cultures, *Journal of Experimental Social Psychology* 39, no. 5 (2003): 476–82; T. Takata, "Self-Enhancement and Self-Criticism in Japanese Culture: An Experimental Analysis, *Journal of Cross-Cultural Psychology* 34, no. 5 (2003): 542–51; and T. Yamagishi, H. Hashimoto, K. S. Cook, T. Kiyonari, M. Shinada, N. Mifune, K. Inukai, H. Takagishi, Y. Horita, and Y. Li, "Modesty in Self-Presentation: A Comparison between the USA and Japan, *Asian Journal of Social Psychology* 15, no. 1 (2012): 60–68.

20. See M. H. Teicher, J. A. Samson, A. Polcari, and C. E. McGreenery, "Sticks, Stones, and Hurtful Words: Relative Effects of Various Forms of Childhood Maltreatment," *American Journal of Psychiatry* 163, no. 6 (2006): 993–1000; and A. R. Tyrka, M. C. Wyche, M. M. Kelly, L. H. Price, and L. L. Carpenter, "Childhood Maltreatment and Adult Personality Disorder Symptoms: Influence of Maltreatment Type," *Psychiatry Research* 165, no. 3 (2009): 281–87.

21. N. Sachs-Ericsson, E. Verona, T. Joiner, and K. J. Preacher, "Parental Verbal Abuse and the Mediating Role of Self-Criticism in Adult Internalizing Disorders," *Journal of Affective Disorders* 93, nos. 1–3 (2006): 71–78.

22. E. Colvin, B. Gardner, P. Labelle, and D. Santor, "The Automaticity of Positive and Negative Thinking: A Scoping Review of Mental Habits," *Cognitive Therapy and Research* (2021): 2.

23. B. Verplanken, O. Friborg, C. E. Wang, D. Trafimow, and K. Woolf, "Mental Habits: Metacognitive Reflection on Negative

Self-Thinking," *Journal of Personality and Social Psychology* 92, no. 3 (2007): 526–41.

24. Verplanken et al., "Mental Habits," 526-41.

25. J. G. Breines and S. Chen, "Self-Compassion Increases Self-Improvement Motivation," *Personality and Social Psychology Bulletin* 38, no. 9 (2012): 1133–43.

26. See Y. Kurebayashi, "Self-Compassion and Nursing Competency among Japanese Psychiatric Nurses," *Perspectives in Psychiatric Care* 57, no. 3 (2020): 1009–18; F. Pires, S. S. Lacerda, J. B. Balardin, B. Portes, P. R. Tobo, C. Barrichello, E. Amaro Jr., and E. H. Kozasa, "Self-Compassion Is Associated with Less Stress and Depression and Greater Attention and Brain Response to Affective Stimuli in Women Managers," *BMC Women's Health* 18 no. 1 (2018): 195.

27. M. Stein and S. Cacciola, "Why Do the Warriors Dominate the 3rd Quarter? Consider Their Halftime Drill," *New York Times*, May 31, 2018.

28. D. Siegel, *Pocket Guide to Interpersonal Neurobiology: An Integrative Handbook of the Mind* (New York: W. W. Norton & Co., 2012), 21.

29. T. Nhat Hanh, *No Mud, No Lotus: The Art of Transforming Suffering* (Berkeley, CA: Parallax Press, 2014), 20.

30. Thomas Moore, *Care of the Soul: A Guide for Cultivating Depth and Sacredness in Everyday Life* (New York: Harper-Collins, 1992).

31. Michelle Obama, *Becoming* (New York: Crown, 2018), 284.

32. Obama, *Becoming*, 320.

33. Daniel Goleman and Richard J. Davidson, *Altered Traits: Science Reveals How Meditation Changes Your Mind, Brain, and Body* (New York: Avery, 2017).

34. A. Diedrich, S. G. Hofmann, P. Cuijpers, and M. Berking, "Self-Compassion Enhances the Efficacy of Explicit Cognitive Reappraisal as an Emotion Regulation Strategy in Individuals with Major Depressive Disorder," *Behaviour Research and Therapy* 82 (2016): 1–10.

Chapter 1. Inhale, My Friend; Exhale, My Friend

1. Eckhart Tolle, "One Conscious Breath," 2020, www.youtube. com/watch?v=3cqri927FKk&ab_channel=GratitudeSeeds.
2. N. A. Paul, S. J. Stanton, J. M. Greeson, M. J. Smoski, and L. Wang, "Psychological and Neural Mechanisms of Trait Mindfulness in Reducing Depression Vulnerability," *Social Cognitive and Affective Neuroscience* 8, no. 1 (2013): 56–64.
3. C. G. Ng, K. T. Lai, S. B. Tan, A. H. Sulaiman, and N. Z. Zainal, "The Effect of 5 Minutes of Mindful Breathing to the Perception of Distress and Physiological Responses in Palliative Care Cancer Patients: A Randomized Controlled Study," *Journal of Palliative Medicine* 19, no. 9 (2016): 917–24.
4. A. Doll, B. K. Hölzel, S. Mulej Bratec, C. C. Boucard, X. Xie, A. M. Wohlschläger, and C. Sorg, "Mindful Attention to Breath Regulates Emotions via Increased Amygdala-Prefrontal Cortex Connectivity," *NeuroImage* 134 (2016): 305–13; F. Zeidan, K. T. Martucci, R. A. Kraft, J. G. McHaffie, and R. C. Coghill, "Neural Correlates of Mindfulness Meditation-Related Anxiety Relief," *Social Cognitive and Affective Neuroscience* 9, no. 6 (2014): 751–59.
5. Zeidan et al., "Neural Correlates," 751–59.
6. T. Nhat Hanh, "How Do I Love Myself?" July 6, 2014, YouTube Video, 13:33, www.youtube.com/watch?v=gMoRtJhVoxc&ab_channel=PlumVillage.
7. S. Selassie, "Bio," Liberate (website), retrieved July 17, 2021, https://liberatemeditation.com/teachers/sebene-selassie.
8. For example, see V. Perciavalle, M. Blandini, P. Fecarotta, A. Buscemi, D. Di Corrado, L. Bertolo, F. Fichera, and M. Coco, "The Role of Deep Breathing on Stress," *Neurological Sciences* 38, no. 3 (2017): 451–58.
9. Marcus Raichle interviewed by Svend Davanger, "The Brain's Default Mode Network—What Does It Mean to Us?" *The Meditation Blog*, www.themeditationblog.com/the-brains-default-mode-network-what-does-it-mean-to-us/, March 9, 2015.

10. P. Gilbert, K. McEwan, M. Matos, and A. Rivis, "Fears of Compassion: Development of Three Self-Report Measures," *Psychology and Psychotherapy: Theory, Research and Practice* 84 (2011): 239–55.

11. T. Nhat Hanh, *The Path of Emancipation: Talks from a 21-Day Mindfulness Retreat* (Berkeley, CA: Parallax Press, 2000), 36.

12. Thanissaro Bhikkhu, *Anapanasati Sutta: Mindfulness of Breathing*, translated from the Pali by Thanissaro Bhikkhu, 2006, retrieved July 19, 2021, from www.accesstoinsight.org/tipitaka/mn/mn.118.than.html.

13. T. Nhat Hanh, *Breathe! You Are Alive: Sutra on the Full Awareness of Breathing* (Berkeley, CA: Parallax Press, 1996), 24.

14. Nhat Hanh, *The Path of Emancipation*, 36.

15. I recommend Larry Rosenberg's *Breath by Breath: The Liberating Practice of Insight Meditation* (Boston: Shambhala, 1998); Ajahn Brahm's *Mindfulness, Bliss, and Beyond* (Somerville, MA: Wisdom Publications, 2006); Buddhadasa Bhikku's *Mindfulness with Breathing: A Manual for Serious Beginners* (Boston, MA: Wisdom Publications, 1988); or T. Nhat Hanh's *Breathe! You Are Alive: Sutra on the Full Awareness of Breathing* (Berkeley, CA: Parallax Press, 1996).

Chapter 2. Spot the Success

1. J. K. Gollan, D. Hoxha, K. Hunnicutt-Ferguson, C. J. Norris, L. Rosebrock, L. Sankin, and J. Cacioppo, "Twice the Negativity Bias and Half the Positivity Offset: Evaluative Responses to Emotional Information in Depression," *Journal of Behavior Therapy and Experimental Psychiatry* 52 (2016): 166–70.

2. J. Kabat-Zinn, *Full Catastrophe Living: Using the Wisdom of Your Body and Mind to Face Stress, Pain, and Illness*, rev. ed. (New York: Bantam Books, 2013), xlix.

3. Public Broadcasting System, *Healing and the Mind with Bill Moyers*, 1993, YouTube video, 1:25:55, June 26, 2017, https://miamimindfulness.com/2017/06/26/bill-moyers-interview-w-jon-kabat-zinn-on-the-mbsr-program-pbs-1993/.

4. C. Marske, S. Shah, A. Chavira, C. Hedberg, R. Fullmer, C. J. Clark, O. Pipitone, and P. Kaiser, "Mindfulness-Based Stress Reduction in the Management of Chronic Pain and Its Co-morbid Depression," *Journal of the American Osteopathic Association* 120, no. 9 (2020): 575–81; and M. Janssen, Y. Heerkens, W. Kuijer, B. van der Heijden, and J. Engels, "Effects of Mindfulness-Based Stress Reduction on Employees' Mental Health: A Systematic Review," *PloS One* 13, no. 1 (2018): e0191332.

5. C. L. Gordon, R. A. M. Arnette, and R. E. Smith, "Have You Thanked Your Spouse Today? Felt and Expressed Gratitude among Married Couples," *Personality and Individual Differences* 50, no. 3 (2011): 339–43; and Y. Park, E. A. Impett, G. Mac-Donald, and E. P. Lemay Jr., "Saying 'Thank You': Partners' Expressions of Gratitude Protect Relationship Satisfaction and Commitment from the Harmful Effects of Attachment Insecurity," *Journal of Personality and Social Psychology* 117, no. 4 (2019): 773–806.

6. M. Ross and F. Sicoly, "Egocentric Biases in Availability and Attribution," *Journal of Personality and Social Psychology* 50 no. 3 (1979): 322–36.

7. P. Reps and M. Senzaki, *Zen Flesh, Zen Bones: A Collection of Zen and Pre-Zen Writings* (Tokyo: Tuttle Publishing, 1957).

8. A. J. Crum and E. J. Langer, "Mind-Set Matters: Exercise and the Placebo Effect," *Psychological Science* 18, no. 2 (2007): 165–71.

9. C. Heath and D. Heath, *Switch: How to Change Things When Change Is Hard* (New York: Broadway Books 2010).

10. J. P. Jamieson, W. B. Mendes, E. Blackstock, and T. Schmader, "Turning the Knots in Your Stomach into Bows: Reappraising Arousal Improves Performance on the GRE," *Journal of Experimental Social Psychology* 46, no. 1 (2010): 208–12.

11. Jamieson et al., "Turning the Knots in Your Stomach into Bows," 208–12.

12. J. P. Jamieson, B. J. Peters, E. J. Greenwood, and A. J. Altose, "Reappraising Stress Arousal Improves Performance and

Reduces Evaluation Anxiety in Classroom Exam Situations," *Social Psychological and Personality Science* 7, no. 6 (2016): 579–87.

13. A. W. Brooks, "Get Excited: Reappraising Pre-performance Anxiety as Excitement," *Journal of Experimental Psychology* 143, no. 3 (2014): 1144–58.

14. S. G. Hofmann, S. Heering, A. T. Sawyer, and A. Asnaani, "How to Handle Anxiety: The Effects of Reappraisal, Acceptance, and Suppression Strategies on Anxious Arousal," *Behaviour Research and Therapy* 47 (2009): 389–94.

15. P. R. Goldin, C. A. Moodie, and J. J. Gross, "Acceptance versus Reappraisal: Behavioral, Autonomic, and Neural Effects," *Cognitive, Affective and Behavioral Neuroscience* 19, no. 4 (2019): 927–44.

16. J. J. Gross, "Antecedent- and Response-Focused Emotion Regulation: Divergent Consequences for Experience, Expression, and Physiology," *Journal of Personality and Social Psychology* 74, no. 1 (1998): 224–37.

17. A. P. DePrince, A. T. Chu, and A. S. Pineda, "Links between Specific Posttrauma Appraisals and Three Forms of Trauma-Related Distress," *Psychological Trauma: Theory, Research, Practice, and Policy* 3, no. 4 (2011): 430–41; and P. A. Resick, C. M. Monson, and K. M. Chard, *Cognitive Processing Therapy: Veteran/Military Version: Therapist and Patient Materials Manual* (Washington, DC: Department of Veterans Affairs, 2014).

18. A. A. Ellis, R. D. V. Nixon, and P. Williamson, "The Effects of Social Support and Negative Appraisals on Acute Stress Symptoms and Depression in Children and Adolescents," *The British Journal of Clinical Psychology* 48, pt. 4 (2009): 347–61

19. R. A. Bryant and R. M. Guthrie, "Maladaptive Self-Appraisals Before Trauma Exposure Predict Posttraumatic Stress Disorder," *Journal of Consulting and Clinical Psychology* 75, no. 5 (2007): 812–15.

20. C. G. Martin, L. D. Cromer, A. P. Deprince, and J. J. Freyd, "The Role of Cumulative Trauma, Betrayal, and Appraisals in Understanding Trauma Symptomatology," *Psychological Trauma: Theory, Research, Practice and Policy* 52, no. 2 (2013): 110–18.

21. Resick et al., *Cognitive Processing Therapy.*

22. G. Asmundson, A. S. Thorisdottir, J. W. Roden-Foreman, S. O. Baird, S. M. Witcraft, A. T. Stein, J. Smits, and M. B. Powers, "A Meta-Analytic Review of Cognitive Processing Therapy for Adults with Posttraumatic Stress Disorder," *Cognitive Behaviour Therapy* 48, no. 1 (2019): 1–14.

23. J. A. Schumm, B. D. Dickstein, K. H. Walter, G. P. Owens, and K. M. Chard, "Changes in Posttraumatic Cognitions Predict Changes in Posttraumatic Stress Disorder Symptoms during Cognitive Processing Therapy," *Journal of Consulting and Clinical Psychology* 83, no. 6 (2015): 1161–66.

24. J. T. Moskowitz, J. R. Hult, C. Bussolari, and M. Acree, "What Works in Coping with HIV? A Meta-Analysis with Implications for Coping with Serious Illness," *Psychological Bulletin* 135 (2009): 121–41.

25. N. Garnefski and V. Kraaij, "Relationships between Cognitive Emotion Regulation Strategies and Depressive Symptoms: A Comparative Study of Five Specific Samples," *Personality and Individual Differences* 40 (2006): 1659–69; and A. S. Troy, F. H. Wilhelm, A. J. Shallcross, and I. B. Mauss, "Seeing the Silver Lining: Cognitive Reappraisal Ability Moderates the Relationship between Stress and Depressive Symptoms," *Emotion* 10 (2010): 783–95.

26. A. Dekker, "Why You Should Make a 'Done List,'" January 7, 2020, https://andreadekker.com/making-a-done-list/.

27. M. G. Adler and N. S. Fagley, "Appreciation: Individual Differences in Finding Value and Meaning as a Unique Predictor of Subjective Well-Being," *Journal of Personality* 73 (2005): 79–114.

28. N. S. Fagley, "Appreciation Uniquely Predicts Life Satisfaction above Demographics, the Big 5 Personality Factors, and Gratitude," *Personality and Individual Differences* 53, no. 1 (2012): 59–63.

29. C. Murphy, "When Things Go Right: Dealing with Success with Humility," Tiny Buddha, retrieved February 4, 2021, https://tinybuddha.com/blog/when-things-go-right-dealing-with-success-with-humility/.

30. L. Brown, "Gratitude Lists Are B.S. — It Was an 'Ingratitude' List That Saved Me," *Good Housekeeping*, August 4, 2017, retrieved August 19, 2021, www.goodhousekeeping.com/life/a45386/gratitude-lists-dont-work/.

31. M. T. Boden, M. O. Bonn-Miller, T. B. Kashdan, J. Alvarez, and J. J. Gross, "The Interactive Effects of Emotional Clarity and Cognitive Reappraisal in Posttraumatic Stress Disorder," *Journal of Anxiety Disorders* 26, no. 1 (2012): 233–38.

32. S. Boehme, S. C. Biehl, and A. Mühlberger, "Effects of Differential Strategies of Emotion Regulation," *Brain Sciences* 9, no. 9 (2019): 225.

33. J. J. Flynn, T. Hollenstein, and A. Mackey, "The Effect of Suppressing and Not Accepting Emotions on Depressive Symptoms: Is Suppression Different for Men and Women?" *Personality and Individual Differences* 49, no. 6 (2010): 582–86.

34. Hofmann et al., "How to Handle Anxiety."

Chapter 3. Nonjudgment, or at Least a Lot Less Judgment

1. B. Chin, J. Slutsky, J. Raye, and J. D. Creswell, "Mindfulness Training Reduces Stress at Work: A Randomized Controlled Trial," *Mindfulness* 10, no. 4 (2019): 627–38; and B. L. Fredrickson, A. J. Boulton, A. M. Firestine, P. Van Cappellen, S. B. Algoe, M. M. Brantley, S. L. Kim, J. Brantley, and S. Salzberg, "Positive Emotion Correlates of Meditation Practice: A Comparison of Mindfulness Meditation and Loving-Kindness Meditation," *Mindfulness* 8, no. 6 (2017): 1623–33.

2. N. Stephenson, *Fall, or Dodge in Hell* (New York: William Morrow, 2019), 13.

3. G. Ortet, D. Pinazo, D. Walker, S. Gallego, L. Mezquita, and M. I. Ibáñez, "Personality and Nonjudging Make You Happier: Contribution of the Five-Factor Model, Mindfulness Facets and a Mindfulness Intervention to Subjective Well-Being," *PLoS One* 2 (2020).

4. J. T. Quaglia, S. E. Braun, S. P. Freeman, M. A. McDaniel, and K. W. Brown, "Meta-Analytic Evidence for Effects of Mindfulness Training on Dimensions of Self-Reported Dispositional Mindfulness," *Psychological Assessment* 28, no. 7 (2016): 803–18.

5. N. A. Farb, A. K. Anderson, and Z. V. Segal, "The Mindful Brain and Emotion Regulation in Mood Disorders," *Canadian Journal of Psychiatry* 57, no. 2 (2012): 4.

6. H. Poissant, A. Mendrek, N. Talbot, B. Khoury, and J. Nolan, "Behavioral and Cognitive Impacts of Mindfulness-Based Interventions on Adults with Attention-Deficit Hyperactivity Disorder: A Systematic Review," *Behavioural Neurology* (2019).

7. H. A. Rahl, E. K. Lindsay, L. E. Pacilio, K. W. Brown, and J. D. Creswell, "Brief Mindfulness Meditation Training Reduces Mind Wandering: The Critical Role of Acceptance," *Emotion* 17, no. 2 (2017): 224–30.

8. S. E. Sauer-Zavala, E. C. Walsh, T. A. Eisenlohr-Moul, and E. L. B. Lykins, "Comparing Mindfulness-Based Intervention Strategies: Differential Effects of Sitting Meditation, Body Scan, and Mindful Yoga," *Mindfulness* 4, no. 4 (2013): 383–88.

9. L. King, *Writers and Lovers* (New York: Grove Press, 2020), 130.

10. E. Adams and E. Frauenheim, *Reinventing Masculinity: The Liberating Power of Compassion and Connection* (Oakland, CA: Berrett-Koehler Publishers, 2020).

11. A. E. Ramon, L. Guthrie, and N. K. Rochester, "Role of Masculinity in Relationships between Mindfulness, Self-Compassion, and Well-Being in Military Veterans," *Psychology of Men and Masculinities* 21, no. 3 (2020): 357–68.

12. Raichle, "The Brain's Default Mode Network."

13. Y. Luo, F. Kong, S. Qi, X. You, and X. Huang, "Resting-State Functional Connectivity of the Default Mode Network Associated with Happiness," *Social Cognitive and Affective Neuroscience* 11, no. 3 (2016): 516–24.

14. J. Kabat-Zinn, "Jon Kabat-Zinn's 6 Tips for Managing Stress," MasterClass, last updated March 8, 2021, www.masterclass.com/articles/stress-management-tips-from-jon-kabat-zinn#what-happens-in-your-body-when-you-react-to-stress.

15. K. A. Garrison, T. A. Zeffiro, D. Scheinost, R. T. Constable, and J. A. Brewer, "Meditation Leads to Reduced Default Mode Network Activity beyond an Active Task," *Cognitive, Affective and Behavioral Neuroscience* 15, no. 3 (2015): 712–20; and H. J. Scheibner, C. Bogler, T. Gleich, J. D. Haynes, and F. Bermpohl, "Internal and External Attention and the Default Mode Network," *Neuroimage* 148 (2017): 381–89.

16. J. A. Brewer, P. D. Worhunsky, J. R. Gray, Y. Y. Tang, J. Weber, and H. Kober, "Meditation Experience Is Associated with Differences in Default Mode Network Activity and Connectivity," *Proceedings of the National Academy of Sciences of the United States of America* 108, no. 50 (2011): 20254–59.

17. Brewer et al., "Meditation Experience Is Associated with Differences in Default Mode Network Activity and Connectivity"; and Scheibner et al., "Internal and External Attention and the Default Mode Network."

18. See A. Doll, B. K. Hölzel, C. C. Boucard, A. M. Wohlschläger, and C. Sorg, "Mindfulness Is Associated with Intrinsic Functional Connectivity between Default Mode and Salience Networks," *Frontiers in Human Neuroscience* 9 (2015): 461; and W. Hasenkamp and L. W. Barsalou, "Effects of Meditation Experience on Functional Connectivity of Distributed Brain Networks," *Frontiers in Human Neuroscience* 6 (2012): 38.

19. L. Shi, J. Sun, X. Wu, D. Wei, Q. Chen, W. Yang, H. Chen, and J. Qiu, "Brain Networks of Happiness: Dynamic Functional Connectivity among the Default, Cognitive and Salience Net-

works Relates to Subjective Well-Being," *Social Cognitive and Affective Neuroscience* 13, no. 8 (2018): 851–62.

20. Scheibner et al., "Internal and External Attention and the Default Mode Network."

21. Doll et al., "Mindfulness Is Associated with Intrinsic Functional Connectivity."

22. J. H. Jang, W. H. Jung, D. H. Kang, M. S. Byun, S. J. Kwon, C. H. Choi, and J. S. Kwon, "Increased Default Mode Network Connectivity Associated with Meditation," *Neuroscience Letters* 487, no. 3 (2011): 358–62.

23. A. Lueke and B. Gibson, "Mindfulness Meditation Reduces Implicit Age and Race Bias: The Role of Reduced Automaticity of Responding," *Social Psychological and Personality Science* 6, no. 3 (2015): 284–91.

24. "Sharon Salzberg Returns—You Made It Weird with Pete Holmes," retrieved August 24, 2021, from www.rickhanson. net/see-beings-not-bodies/.

25. "You Made It Weird Podcast with Pete Holmes," March 18, 2020, www.sharonsalzberg.com/you-made-it-weird-podcast-with-pete-holmes/.

Chapter 4. Fail Forward, or Act Before You Think

1. S. Krimmel, personal communication, March 4, 2020.

2. See M. Ciharova, T. A. Furukawa, O. Efthimiou, E. Karyotaki, C. Miguel, H. Noma, A. Cipriani, H. Riper, and P. Cuijpers, "Cognitive Restructuring, Behavioral Activation and Cognitive-Behavioral Therapy in the Treatment of Adult Depression: A Network Meta-Analysis," *Journal of Consulting and Clinical Psychology* 89, no. 6 (2021): 563–74; H. Imai, M. Yamada, M. Inagaki, N. Watanabe, B. Chino, A. Mantani, and T. A. Furukawa, "Behavioral Activation Contributed to the Total Reduction of Depression Symptoms in the Smartphone-Based Cognitive Behavioral Therapy: A Secondary Analysis of a Randomized, Controlled Trial," *Innovations in Clinical*

Neuroscience 17, no. 79 (2020): 21–25; D. A. Richards, D. Ekers, D. McMillan, R. S. Taylor, S. Byford, F. C. Warren, B. Barrett, P. A. Farrand, S. Gilbody, W. Kuyken, H. O'Mahen, E. R. Watkins, K. A. Wright, S. D. Hollon, N. Reed, S. Rhodes, E. Fletcher, and K. Finning, "Cost and Outcome of Behavioural Activation versus Cognitive Behavioural Therapy for Depression (COBRA): A Randomised, Controlled, Non-Inferiority Trial," *Lancet* 388, no. 10047 (2016): 871–80; W. Saisanan Na Ayudhaya, N. Pityaratstian, and W. Jiamjarasrangsi, "Effectiveness of Behavioral Activation in Treating Thai Older Adults with Subthreshold Depression Residing in the Community," *Clinical Interventions in Aging* 15 (2020): 2363–74; and A. W. Wagner, M. Jakupcak, H. M. Kowalski, J. N. Bittinger, and S. Golshan, "Behavioral Activation as a Treatment for Posttraumatic Stress Disorder among Returning Veterans: A Randomized Trial," *Psychiatric Services* 70, no. 10 (2019): 867–73.

3. L. C. Larabie, "To What Extent Do Smokers Plan Quit Attempts?" *Tobacco Control* 14 (2005): 425–428.

4. J. Giménez-Meseguer, J. Tortosa-Martínez, and J. M. Cortell-Tormo, "The Benefits of Physical Exercise on Mental Disorders and Quality of Life in Substance Use Disorders Patients: Systematic Review and Meta-Analysis," *International Journal of Environmental Research and Public Health* 17, no. 10 (2020): 3680; M. Grasdalsmoen, H. R. Eriksen, K. J. Lonning, and B. Sivertsen, "Physical Exercise, Mental Health Problems, and Suicide Attempts in University Students," *BMC Psychiatry* 20, no. 1 (2020): 175; and I. Kim, and J. Ahn, "The Effect of Changes in Physical Self-Concept through Participation in Exercise on Changes in Self-Esteem and Mental Well-Being," *International Journal of Environmental Research and Public Health* 18, no. 10 (2021): 5224.

5. For example, see K. A. Kaufman, C. R. Glass, and D. B Arnkoff, "Evaluation of Mindful Sport Performance Enhancement (MSPE): A New Approach to Promote Flow in Athletes," *Journal of Clinical Sport Psychology* 3, no. 4 (2009): 334–56.

6. For example, see C. S. Dweck, "Brainology: Transforming Students' Motivation to Learn," National Association of Independent Schools (2008), www.nais.org/publications/ismagazinearticle.cfm?Item Number=150509.

7. I. Kendi, *How to Be an Antiracist* (New York: One World, 2019), 6. Ellipses in original.

8. C. Dweck, *Mindset: The New Psychology of Success* (New York: Random House, 2006), 256.

9. Dweck, *Mindset*, 235.

10. Q. Cutts, E. Cutts, S. Draper, and P. O'Donnell, "Manipulating Mindset to Positively Influence Introductory Programming Performance," Proceedings of the 41st ACM Technical Symposium on Computer Science Education, 2010.

11. A. J. Martin and H. W. Marsh, "Fear of Failure: Friend or Foe?" *Australian Psychologist* 38 (2003): 31–38.

12. S. Palminteri, M. Khamassi, M. Joffily, and G. Coricelli, "Contextual Modulation of Value Signals in Reward and Punishment Learning," *Nature Communications* 6, (2015).

13. Researchers who study these themes report that children who received "process praise" (encouragement about the quality of their effort and engagement) fared better than children who received "person praise" (feedback about a supposed "fixed" quality, such as "you're so smart"). For instance, children who received process praise are more likely to stick to a task, even when it gets challenging—and over time, that persistence seems to generalize into feelings of competence and into willingness to try, to fail, and to take risks. Conversely, even a small amount of generic praise seems to reduce motivation; e.g., see S. R. Zentall and B. J. Morris, "'Good Job, You're Therefore Smart': The Effects of Inconsistency of Praise Type on Young Children's Motivation," *Journal of Experimental Child Psychology* 107, no. 2 (2010): 155–63.

14. As in Cutts et al., "Manipulating Mindset." For instance, one study described changes to teachers' mindsets over a training period of six sessions; a study to change students' mindsets

involved eight workshops; see L. Blackwell, K. Trzesniewski, and C. Dweck, "Implicit Theories of Intelligence Predict Achievement across an Adolescent Transition: A Longitudinal Study and an Intervention," *Child Development* 78, no. 1 (2007): 246–63. Other interventions have methods like mentoring or pen pal programs; see J. Snipes, C. Fancsali, and G. Stoker, *Student Academic Mindset Interventions: A Review of the Current Landscape* (San Francisco, CA: Stupski Foundation 2012).

15. Dweck, *Mindset*, 229.
16. University of Washington Resilience Lab, "Fail Forward" event, April 2018.
17. P. Chödrön, "How to Fail: American Buddhist Nun Pema Chödrön's Advice for Leaning Into the Unknown, *Tricycle*, March 17, 2019.
18. B. Tate, personal communication, May 20, 2020.
19. S. Jaschik, "Sharing the Failures," *Inside Higher Ed*, May 2, 2016, retrieved from insidehighered.com/news/2016/05/02/professors-failure-cv-prompts-discussion-what-constitutes-academic-success on August 10, 2021.
20. O. Babur, "Talking about Failure Is Crucial for Growth. Here's How to Do It Right," *New York Times*, August 17, 2018.
21. M. Nikāya, "The Greater Discourse to Saccaka," retrieved October 14, 2021, https://suttacentral.net/mn36/en/bodhi.
22. University of Washington Resilience Lab, "Fail Forward" event, 2018.

Chapter 5. Training Friendliness with Lovingkindness Meditation

1. R. Jackson, personal communication, email sent June 19, 2021.
2. Bhante Gunaratana, "11 Benefits of Loving-Friendliness Meditation," *Tricycle*, March 30, 2019, https://tricycle.org/trike daily/benefits-loving-friendliness-meditation/.

3. Sharon Salzberg, "Why Loving-Kindness Takes Time," *Mindful*, January 19, 2018, www.mindful.org/loving-kindness-takes-time-sharon-salzberg/.

4. Thanissaro Bhikkhu, "Metta Means Goodwill," 2011, retrieved August 24, 2021, www.accesstoinsight.org/lib/authors/thanissaro/metta_means_goodwill.html.

5. The Amaravati Sangha, "Karaniya Metta Sutta: The Buddha's Words on Loving-Kindness," 2004, retrieved June 14, 2021, https://www.accesstoinsight.org/tipitaka/kn/snp/snp.1.08.amar.html.

6. Sharon Salzberg, *Lovingkindness* (Boston: Shambhala, 1995).

7. Salzberg, *Lovingkindness*, 40.

8. Anālayo, *Compassion and Emptiness in Early Buddhist Meditation* (Cambridge: Windhorse Publications, 2015).

9. Salzberg, "Why Loving-Kindness Takes Time."

10. See J. Galante, I. Galante, M. J. Bekkers, and J. Gallacher, "Effect of Kindness-Based Meditation on Health and Well-Being: A Systematic Review and Meta-Analysis," *Journal of Consulting and Clinical Psychology* 82, no. 6 (2014): 1101–14; S. G. Hofmann, N. Petrocchi, J. Steinberg, M. Lin, K. Arimitsu, S. Kind, A. Mendes, and U. Stangier, "Loving-Kindness Meditation to Target Affect in Mood Disorders: A Proof-of-Concept Study," *Evidence-Based Complementary and Alternative Medicine: eCAM* (2015); D. J. Kearney, C. A. Malte, M. Storms, and T. L. Simpson, "Loving-Kindness Meditation vs. Cognitive Processing Therapy for Posttraumatic Stress Disorder among Veterans: A Randomized Clinical Trial," *Journal of the American Medical Association* 4, no. 4 (2021): e216604; I. Kurdieh, "The Influence of Loving-Kindness Meditation on Everyday Experiences of Being Angry: An Empirical Phenomenological Study" doctoral dissertation, Duquesne University, 2014), https://dsc.duq.edu/etd/794; and T. Totzeck, T. Teismann, S. G. Hofmann, et al., "Loving-Kindness Meditation Promotes Mental Health in University Students," *Mindfulness* 11 (2020): 1623–31.

11. J. W. Carson, F. J. Keefe, T. R. Lynch, K. M. Carson, V. Goli, A. M. Fras, and S. R. Thorp, "Loving-Kindness Meditation for Chronic Low Back Pain: Results from a Pilot Trial," *Journal of Holistic Nursing: Official Journal of the American Holistic Nurses' Association* 23, no. 3 (2005): 287–304.

12. A. A. Wren, R. A. Shelby, M. S. Soo, Z. Huysmans, J. A. Jarosz, and F. J. Keefe, "Preliminary Efficacy of a Lovingkindness Meditation Intervention for Patients Undergoing Biopsy and Breast Cancer Surgery: A Randomized Controlled Pilot Study," *Supportive Care in Cancer: Official Journal of the Multinational Association of Supportive Care in Cancer* 27, no. 9 (2019): 3583–92.

13. See A. Feliu-Soler, J. C. Pascual, M. Elices, A. Martín-Blanco, C. Carmona, A. Cebolla, V. Simón, and J. Soler, "Fostering Self-Compassion and Loving-Kindness in Patients with Borderline Personality Disorder: A Randomized Pilot Study," *Clinical Psychology and Psychotherapy* 24, no. 1 (2017): 278–86; S. Noh and H. Cho, "Psychological and Physiological Effects of the Mindful Lovingkindness Compassion Program on Highly Self-Critical University Students in South Korea," *Frontiers in Psychology* 11 (2020): 585743; B. Shahar, O. Szsepsenwol, S. Zilcha-Mano, N. Haim, O. Zamir, S. Levi-Yeshuvi, and N. Levit-Binnun, "A Wait-List Randomized Controlled Trial of Loving-Kindness Meditation Programme for Self-Criticism," *Clinical Psychology and Psychotherapy* 22, no. 4 (2015): 346–56; and D. T. Weibel, A. S. McClintock, and T. Anderson, "Does Loving-Kindness Meditation Reduce Anxiety? Results from a Randomized Controlled Trial," *Mindfulness* 8, (2017): 565–71.

14. Noh and Cho, "Psychological and Physiological Effects of the Mindful Lovingkindness Compassion Program"; Shahar et al., "A Wait-List Randomized Controlled Trial of Loving-Kindness Meditation Programme for Self-Criticism."

15. J. S. Mascaro, A. Darcher, L. T. Negi, and C. L. Raison, "The Neural Mediators of Kindness-Based Meditation: A Theoretical Model," *Frontiers in Psychology* 6 (2015): 109.

16. H. Kirschner, W. Kuyken, K. Wright, H. Roberts, C. Brejcha, and A. Karl, "Soothing Your Heart and Feeling Connected: A New Experimental Paradigm to Study the Benefits of Self-Compassion," *Clinical Psychological Science: A Journal of the Association for Psychological Science* 7, no. 3 (2019): 545–65.

17. Brewer et al., "Meditation Experience Is Associated with Differences in Default Mode Network Activity and Connectivity."

18. S. B. Johnson, B. L. Goodnight, H. Zhang, I. Daboin, B. Patterson, and N. J. Kaslow, "Compassion-Based Meditation in African Americans: Self-Criticism Mediates Changes in Depression," *Suicide and Life-Threatening Behavior* 48, no. 2 (2018): 160–68.

19. B. L. Fredrickson, M. A. Cohn, K. A. Coffey, J. Pek, and S. M. Finkel, "Open Hearts Build Lives: Positive Emotions, Induced through Loving-Kindness Meditation, Build Consequential Personal Resources," *Journal of Personality and Social Psychology* 95, no. 5 (2008): 1045–62; M. A. Cohn and B. L. Fredrickson, "In Search of Durable Positive Psychology Interventions: Predictors and Consequences of Long-Term Positive Behavior Change," *Journal of Positive Psychology* 5 (2010): 355– 66.

20. U. Sirotina and S. Shchebetenko, "Loving-Kindness Meditation and Compassion Meditation: Do They Affect Emotions in a Different Way?" *Mindfulness* 11, (2020): 2519–30.

21. A. J. Stell and T. Farsides, "Brief Loving-Kindness Meditation Reduces Racial Bias, Mediated by Positive Other-Regarding Emotions," *Motivation and Emotion* 40, no. 1 (2016): 140–47.

22. E. M. Seppälä, C. A. Hutcherson, D. T. Nguyen, J. R. Doty, and J. J. Gross, "Loving-Kindness Meditation: A Tool to Improve Healthcare Provider Compassion, Resilience, and Patient Care," *Journal of Compassionate Health Care* 1 (2014), https://jcompassionatehc.biomedcentral.com/articles/10.1186/s40639-014-0005-9.

23. Kurdieh, "The Influence of Loving-Kindness Meditation on Everyday Experiences of Being Angry."

24. K. W. Brown, "A Phenomenological Study of Loving Kindness Practice in Education Settings," master's thesis, Graduate Department of Curriculum, Teaching, and Learning (CTL), Ontario Institute for Studies in Education University of Toronto (2016), 66.

25. C. A. Hutcherson, E. M. Seppälä, and J. J. Gross, "Loving-Kindness Meditation Increases Social Connectedness," *Emotion* 8, no. 5 (2008): 720–24.

26. See Y. Kang, J. R. Gray, and J. F. Dovidio, "The Nondiscriminating Heart: Lovingkindness Meditation Training Decreases Implicit Intergroup Bias," *Journal of Experimental Psychology: General* 143, no. 3 (2014): 1306–13; M. Hunsinger, R. Livingston, and L. Isbell, "Spirituality and Intergroup Harmony: Meditation and Racial Prejudice," *Mindfulness* 5, no. 2 (2012): 139–44; and Stell and Farsides, "Brief Loving-Kindness Meditation Reduces Racial Bias."

27. See Y. Kang and E. B. Falk, "Neural Mechanisms of Attitude Change toward Stigmatized Individuals: Temporoparietal Junction Activity Predicts Bias Reduction," *Mindfulness* 11, no. 6 (2020): 1378–89; Kang, Gray, and Dovidio, "The Nondiscriminating Heart: Lovingkindness Meditation Training Decreases Implicit Intergroup Bias"; and S. Parks, M. D. Birtel, and R. J. Crisp, "Evidence That a Brief Meditation Exercise Can Reduce Prejudice toward Homeless People" *Social Psychology* 45, no. 6 (2014): 458–65.

28. H. Chen, C. Liu, X. Cao, B. Hong, D. H. Huang, C. Y. Liu, and W. K. Chiou, "Effects of Loving-Kindness Meditation on Doctors' Mindfulness, Empathy, and Communication Skills," *International Journal of Environmental Research and Public Health* 18, no. 8 (2021): 4033; M. Leppma and M. E. Young, "Loving-Kindness Meditation and Empathy: A Wellness Group Intervention for Counseling Students," *Journal of Counseling and Development* 94, no. 3 (2016): 297–305.

29. U. Kreplin, M. Farias, and I. A. Brazil, "The Limited Prosocial Effects of Meditation: A Systematic Review and Meta-Analysis," *Scientific Reports* 8, no. 1 (2018).

30. J. Bankard, "Training Emotion Cultivates Morality: How Loving-Kindness Meditation Hones Compassion and Increases Prosocial Behavior," *Journal of Religion and Health* 54 (2014): 2324–43.

31. Y. Engel, A. Ramesh, and N. Steiner, "Powered by Compassion: The Effect of Loving-Kindness Meditation on Entrepreneurs' Sustainable Decision-Making," *Journal of Business Venturing* 35, no. 6 (2020).

32. Chen et al., "Effects of Loving-Kindness Meditation on Doctors' Mindfulness, Empathy, and Communication Skills."

33. C. K. Germer and K. D. Neff, "Self-Compassion in Clinical Practice," *Journal of Clinical Psychology* 69, no. 8 (2013): 856–67.

34. T. D. Rohrer, "To Love Abundantly: Sharon Salzberg's Journey on the Path," 2020, www.lionsroar.com/to-love-abundantly-sharon-salzbergs-journey-on-the-path/.

35. Brown, "A Phenomenological Study of Loving Kindness Practice in Education Settings," 62.

36. A. Sumedho, "Nothing Is Left Out: The Practice of Loving-kindness," in *Voices of Insight: Teachers of Buddhism in the West Share Their Wisdom, Stories, and Experiences of Insight Meditation*, edited by Sharon Salzberg (Boston: Shambhala, 1999), 171.

37. Brown, "A Phenomenological Study of Loving Kindness Practice in Education Settings," 62.

38. The researchers (Emanuel et al.) asked 3,185 participants to what extent they agreed with these two statements: "When I feel threatened or anxious I find myself thinking about my values," and "When I feel threatened or anxious I find myself thinking about my strengths." Most people did, in fact, agree that they engaged in this kind of spontaneous thinking, those who agreed more strongly with the questions also reported

higher levels of hope, optimism, and health, and lower levels of sadness and anger. Great! However, we still don't know exactly what kinds of affirmative thoughts people were engaging. Were they statements or phrases? Did making the affirmations lead people to feel better? Or were people with higher levels of well-being also just generally more in tune with their personal strengths and values? See A. S. Emanuel, J. L. Howell, J. M. Taber, R. A. Ferrer, W. M. Klein, and P. R. Harris, "Spontaneous Self-Affirmation Is Associated with Psychological Well-Being: Evidence from a US National Adult Survey Sample," *Journal of Health Psychology* 23, no. 1 (2018): 95–102.

39. R. W. Robins and J. S. Beer, "Positive Illusions about the Self: Short-Term Benefits and Long-Term Costs," *Journal of Personality and Social Psychology* 80, no. 2 (2001): 340–52.

40. See W. Duan, "The Benefits of Personal Strengths in Mental Health of Stressed Students: A Longitudinal Investigation," *Quality of Life Research: An International Journal of Quality of Life Aspects of Treatment, Care and Rehabilitation* 25, no. 11 (2016): 2879–88; D. K. Sherman, D. P. Bunyan, J. D. Creswell, and L. M. Jaremka, "Psychological Vulnerability and Stress: The Effects of Self-Affirmation on Sympathetic Nervous System Responses to Naturalistic Stressors," *Health Psychology: Official Journal of the Division of Health Psychology, American Psychological Association* 28, no. 5 (2009): 554–62; and A. Springer, A. Venkatakrishnan, S. Mohan, L. Nelson, M. Silva, and P. Pirolli, "Leveraging Self-Affirmation to Improve Behavior Change: A Mobile Health App Experiment. *JMIR mHealth and uHealth* 6, no. 7 (2018): e157.

41. Brown, "A Phenomenological Study of Loving Kindness Practice in Education Settings," 63.

42. A. Lolla, "Mantras Help the General Psychological Well-Being of College Students: A Pilot Study," *Journal of Religion and Health* 57, no. 1 (2018): 110–19.

43. See J. D. Lane, J. E. Seskevich, and C. F. Pieper, "Brief Meditation Training Can Improve Perceived Stress and Negative Mood," *Alternative Therapies in Health and Medicine* 13, no. 1 (2007): 38–44; and S. Leary, K. Weingart, R. Topp, and J. Bormann, "The Effect of Mantram Repetition on Burnout and Stress among VA Staff, *Workplace Health and Safety* 66, no. 3 (2018): 120–28.

44. J. N. Crawford, A. M. Talkovsky, J. E. Bormann, and A. J. Lang, "Targeting Hyperarousal: Mantram Repetition Program for PTSD in US Veterans," *European Journal of Psychotraumatology* 10, no. 1 (2019).

45. See J. E. Bormann, A. L. Gifford, M. Shively, T. L. Smith, L. Redwine, A. Kelly, S. Becker, M. Gershwin, P. Bone, and W. Belding, "Effects of Spiritual Mantram Repetition on HIV Outcomes: A Randomized Controlled Trial," *Journal of Behavioral Medicine* 29, no. 4 (2006): 359–76; and Lolla, "Mantras Help the General Psychological Well-Being of College Students."

46. C. Liu, H. Chen, C. Y. Liu, R. T. Lin, and W. K. Chiou, "The Effect of Loving-Kindness Meditation on Flight Attendants' Spirituality, Mindfulness and Subjective Well-Being," *Healthcare* (Basel, Switzerland) 8, no. 2 (2020): 174.

47. I. Csaszar, J. R. Curry, and R. E. Lastrapes, "Effects of Loving Kindness Meditation on Student Teachers' Reported Levels of Stress and Empathy," *Teacher Education Quarterly* 45 (2018): 93–116.

48. For example, see C. L. Orellana-Rios, L. Radbruch, M. Kern, Y. U. Regel, A. Anton, S. Sinclair, and S. Schmidt, "Mindfulness and Compassion-Oriented Practices at Work Reduce Distress and Enhance Self-Care of Palliative Care Teams: A Mixed-Method Evaluation of an 'On the Job' Program," *BMC Palliative Care* 17, no. 1 (2017): 3.

49. Brown, "A Phenomenological Study of Loving Kindness Practice in Education Settings," 64, 65.

50. Brown 71.

51. Orellana-Rios et al., "Mindfulness and Compassion-Oriented Practices at Work Reduce Distress and Enhance Self-Care of Palliative Care Teams"

52. L. Richmond, *Work as a Spiritual Practice: A Practical Buddhist Approach to Inner Growth and Satisfaction on the Job* (New York: Broadway Books, 2020), 39, 40.

Chapter 6. Allowing All Feelings, Skillfully

1. "The One you Feed: Practical Wisdom for a Better Life," Susan Piver interview, January 13, 2015, www.oneyoufeed.net/susan-piver/.

2. J. Goldstein, *Mindfulness: A Practical Guide to Awakening* (Boulder, CO: Sounds True, 2016), 351.

3. Anyen Rinpoche, "The 4 Noble Truths of Emotional Suffering," *Lion's Roar*, April 12, 2021, www.lionsroar.com/the-4-noble-truths-of-emotional-suffering/.

4. M. M. Linehan, *DBT Skills Training Handouts and Worksheets*, 2nd ed. (New York: The Guilford Press, 2015).

5. A. Clover, "How to Feel Emotions (Because Most of Us Were Never Taught)," *Medium*, February 26, 2017, https://medium.com/@stronginsideout/how-to-feel-emotions-because-most-of-us-were-never-taught-a5eb83dff369.

6. M. M. Linehan, *DBT Skills Training Handouts and Worksheets* (New York: Guilford Press, 2015).

7. K. Neff, *Self-Compassion: The Proven Power of Being Kind to Yourself* (New York: HarperCollins, 2011).

8. J. Kullander, "Sitting in the Fire: Pema Chödrön on Turning Towards Pain," *The Sun*, January 2005, www.thesunmagazine.org/issues/349/sitting-in-the-fire.

9. N. T. Van Dam, S. C. Sheppard, J. P. Forsyth, and M. Earleywine, "Self-Compassion Is a Better Predictor Than Mindfulness of Symptom Severity and Quality of Life in Mixed Anxiety and Depression," *Journal of Anxiety Disorders* 25, no. 1 (2011): 123–30.

10. A. D. Mosewich, K. C. Kowalski, C. M. Sabston, W. A. Sedgwick, and J. L. Tracy, "Self-Compassion: A Potential Resource for Young Women Athletes," *Journal of Sport and Exercise Psychology* 33, no. 1 (2011): 103–23.

11. K. D. Neff and C. K. Germer, "A Pilot Study and Randomized Controlled Trial of the Mindful Self-Compassion Program," *Journal of Clinical Psychology* 69, no. 1 (2013): 28–44.

12. L. Rosenberg, *Breath by Breath: The Liberating Practice of Insight Meditation* (Boston: Shambhala, 2004), 21–22.

13. G. Feldman, J. Greeson, and J. Senville, "Differential Effects of Mindful Breathing, Progressive Muscle Relaxation, and Loving-Kindness Meditation on Decentering and Negative Reactions to Repetitive Thoughts," *Behaviour Research and Therapy* 48, no. 10 (2010): 1002–11.

14. D. D. Colgan, H. Wahbeh, M. Pleet, K. Besler, and M. Christopher, "A Qualitative Study of Mindfulness among Veterans with Posttraumatic Stress Disorder: Practices Differentially Affect Symptoms, Aspects of Well-Being, and Potential Mechanisms of Action," *Journal of Evidence-Based Complementary and Alternative Medicine* 22, no. 3 (2017): 482–93.

15. Nhat Hanh, *No Mud, No Lotus*, 44.

16. H. Mitmansgruber, T. Beck, S. Höfer, and G. Schüssler, "When You Don't Like What You Feel: Experiential Avoidance, Mindfulness and Meta-Emotion in Emotion Regulation," *Personality and Individual Differences* 46 (2009): 448–53.

17. S. G. Hofmann, "The Pursuit of Happiness and Its Relationship to the Meta-Experience of Emotions and Culture," *Australian Psychologist* 48, no. 2 (2013): 94–97.

18. D. Young, personal communication, email, August 31, 2021.

19. "La Sarmiento—Find the Dharma in Everything!" June 14, 2013, www.youtube.com/watch?v=k23CGplBLoo&ab_channel=TaraBrach.

20. B. Q. Ford, P. Lam, O. P. John, and I. B. Mauss, "The Psychological Health Benefits of Accepting Negative Emotions and Thoughts: Laboratory, Diary, and Longitudinal Evidence," *Journal of Personality and Social Psychology* 115, no. 6 (2018): 1075–92.

21. L. Campbell-Sills, D. H. Barlow, T. A. Brown, and S. G. Hofmann, "Effects of Suppression and Acceptance on Emotional Responses of Individuals with Anxiety and Mood Disorders," *Behaviour Research and Therapy* 44, no. 9 (2006): 1251–63, https://doi.org/10.1016/j.brat.2005.10.001.

22. D. R. Evans and S. C. Segestrom, "Why Do Mindful People Worry Less?" *Cognitive Therapy and Research* 35, no. 6 (2011): 505–10.

23. Ford et al., "The Psychological Health Benefits of Accepting Negative Emotions and Thoughts."

24. L. G. Kiken and N. J. Shook, "Does Mindfulness Attenuate Thoughts Emphasizing Negativity, but Not Positivity?" *Journal of Research in Personality* 53 (2014): 22–30.

INDEX

range of, 25–26, 179, 203
secondary, 205–7
styles of relating with,
179–80
taboo in expressing, 46–47
See also feelings
Evans, Daniel, 209
exercise, physical, 53
behavioral activation of,
123–25
health self-talk as, 10–11
mental workouts and, 27
reframing physical labor as,
70–71
exposure therapy, 203–4

"Fail Forward" event, 139
failure, 218
author's experience with,
127–28
cultural views toward, 125
fear of, 117–18, 119
growth mindsets and, 133
misinterpreting events as,
129–30
overidentifying with,
135–37
reflecting on, 140–41
sharing, 137–40
tolerating, 120, 125, 127–28
Fall (Stephenson), 92
Farsides, Tom, 158
fear, 194
allowing, 208
of failure, 117–18, 119

lovingkindness as
protection from, 143, 145
of self-compassion, 42
feelings
accepting, 75–77
author's experience with,
177–78, 181–82, 190–91,
209–11, 212–13
and behavior, relationship
between, 118–19, 122–23
challenging, needing to
allow, 214–15
lovingkindness meditation
and, 163
naming, 22
non-identifying with, 201
nonjudgment toward,
90, 93–94, 100–101,
107–8
observing, 23–24
overanalyzing, 184,
185–86
reflections on, 215–16
restricting, 181–83
self-compassion toward,
197–98
skimming or diving deeply,
207–8
unpleasant, criticism of,
25–26
See also emotions
First Noble Truth, 197. *See also*
suffering
fixed mindset, 130–32, 186–87,
189–90